For Diane,
w/ Warm Wishes,

Tim

2-20-2007

PRAISE FOR
REED CITY BOY

"For anyone who has ever thought about living in a small town–
where most people, it's true, do know your name–Tim Bazzett has
written the perfect book. For those who grew up in small towns,
in places like Reed City (where I was born), this tale is a
reminder of those lost spring afternoons when the redwing
blackbirds called down by the river, and the smell of the creosote
bridge was in the air, with your whole life ahead of you. This
book is funny, poignant, and blazingly honest."

Doug Stanton
Best Selling Author of *In Harm's Way*

"Bazzett tells all with a witty, sometimes hilarious, style so often
missing from memoir writing. ... A very American boy's life [in]
whimsical essays written with a sense of joy and pride. ... This is
the kind of book I wish my dad or grandfather had written. I
would know them better now."

Elizabeth Kane Buzzelli
Traverse City Record-Eagle

"'Don't tell Mom, OK?' In *Reed City Boy* Tim Bazzett tells all,
making his parents proud and leaving his readers anxiously
awaiting his next book, which we certainly hope will not be his
last."

Amy J. Van Ooyen
Author of *Transplants*
and Michigan's U.P. Writer of the Year

"It ought to be required reading for every self-absorbed, video game-addicted, non-chore performing youngster ... *Reed City Boy* captures a certain bygone warmth. ... It honors growing up in small-town America [and depicts] a life that might be defined as a melding of Opie, Beaver and Dobie."

Tom Rademacher
Grand Rapids Press

"Bazzett manages to capture the magic and mystery as well as all the quirks and foibles of growing up in Small Town U.S.A. ... This is a fun book! Well worth the read."

Jim Crees
Pioneer News Network

"The best autobiography I have read in years. ... Paints a picture with a fine artist's brush. ... *Reed City Boy* has universal appeal [and] could easily become a best-seller."

Dr. Maury Dean
Pop Musicologist and author of *Rock and Roll Gold Rush* and *The Rock Revolution*

"A wonderful, touching and honest memoir that will make many smile in empathy as they remember the tortured rites of adolescence. ... A terrific read. I can't wait for the sequel!"

Dr. Neil A. Patten
Ferris State University Professor of Communications

"Delightful! ... Touching, funny, and infused with a love of family, friends and, certainly, Reed City. ... Refreshingly devoid of the usual anger and angst associated with memories of one's youth. ... Write on!"

Dr. Thomas Gordon
Director of Human Services for Oakland County, Michigan

"Thank you for Reed City Boy ... (a) delightful book. It is a fine addition to my library."

Jennifer M. Granholm
Governor of Michigan

"A real piece of American history ... Very well done: honest and frank and very Midwestern (and from me that's praise)."
   Samuel Hynes
   Professor Emeritus of Literature at Princeton University and author of *The Growing Seasons* and *Flights of Passage*

"As anyone who has gone to school at Ferris knows, just north of Paris is not the city of Rouen, but Reed City. In Reed City Boy, Bazzett pays tribute to the town that shaped him ... And as for his style of sledding? 'I was hospitalized for weeks and couldn't walk for months,' Bazzett confesses. An even worse fate than Jean Shepherd's famously ill-fated Christmas gift of a Red Ryder BB gun!"
   Marc Sheehan
   Crimson & Gold

"A good, honest, and straightforward portrait. ... A touching story."
   Ronald Jager
   author of *Eighty Acres*

"Bazzett shares his memories of growing up in Reed City, attending Catholic boarding school in Grand Rapids in the 1950s and working at the local A&P grocery store."
   Lansing State Journal

"Pays tribute to small town life."
   Cadillac News

ReedCityBoy

J J Bazzett

ReedCityBoy

Timothy James Bazzett

RATHOLE BOOKS

REED CITY BOY

©2004 Timothy James Bazzett

Published by Rathole Books
Reed City, Michigan
www.rathole.com/ReedCityBoy

Publisher's Cataloging-in-Publication Data

    Bazzett, Timothy James.

        Reed City Boy / Timothy James Bazzett. -- 3rd ed. -- Reed City, MI :
        Rathole Books, 2005.

            p. ; cm.
            ISBN: 0-9771119-0-3
            ISBN-13: 978-0-9771119-0-9

                1. Bazzett, Timothy James. 2. Working class--Michigan--
                Biography. 3. Catholics--Michigan--Biography. 4. Michigan--Social
                conditions--1945- I. Title.

            HD8073.B399 B39   2005 2005930345
            362.85/09774--dc22   0508

Printed in the United States of America
10 9 8 7 6 5 4

Cover and interior design by Scott Bazzett
Third Edition: August 2005
Third Paperback Edition: August 2005

To order additional copies send check or money order for $14.95 made payable to TJ Bazzett to:

PO Box 282
Reed City, MI 49677-0282

(Michigan residents add 6% sales tax)

For more information, visit us online at:
www.rathole.com/ReedCityBoy

I consider the days of old,
I remember the years long ago.

– Psalms, 77:5

Potterville 1945. Tim and Mom.

*To Mom and Dad, who provided me
with this mostly happy childhood.
To my wife, Terri, who has put up with
me for 36 years. And to the people and
places of Reed City, past and present.*

Table of Contents

Introduction

I have always loved a good story. When my brothers and I were small, my mother would sit down with us at bedtime and open up our collection of *Grimm's Fairy Tales* or Hans Christian Anderson stories and read to us. Or perhaps it might be a Baba Yaga story from the latest issue of *Jack and Jill*, it didn't matter. Even when the story was about a wicked witch, or poor Hansel and Gretel lost in a dark woods, we would still feel safe and secure, sitting in a row on the sofa in our pajamas, tucked up tight against each other with Mom in the middle.

I don't remember my father reading to us much, but I'm sure he did on occasion. But I do remember that when my boys were very young and Mom and Dad would come to visit, he loved to sit down with Jeff and Scott on his lap and read them one of their favorite books, like *The Little Engine that Could*, or *Scuffy the Tugboat*. But what the boys loved best was when Dad would tell them "the puppy story."

"The puppy story" was probably half imagined and half real. When I was little, Dad's parents, my Grandma and Grandpa Bazzett, lived on a farm near Wayland, south of Grand Rapids. They had a dog named Queenie, a Springer Spaniel who was Grandma's special pet and had a whole repertoire of tricks she could perform. She could roll over, play dead, sit up and shake hands – all the usual dog tricks. But the one my brothers and I loved best was "the cracker trick." Grandma would put Queenie into a sit, then she would carefully balance a small square of saltine cracker on the dog's nose. Queenie would sit quivering with cross-eyed anticipation while Grandma slowly counted to three, and on the "three" Queenie would jerk her head up, flipping the cracker into the air and then snatch it and crunch it noisily up. Then she would sit licking her chops, hoping we'd want her to do it again. And of course we always did. Grandma would have to place a limit on how many "cracker tricks" we could watch, since Queenie was already rather old and overweight by the time I met her.

Well, Queenie was in the puppy story that Dad told to Jeff and Scott, and she did her regular tricks and that special "cracker trick" too. Then Dad would tell about the time Queenie had puppies. And every time he told the story the number of puppies and their names would vary. It might be four puppies in one telling and eight or nine in another. And the changing names were perhaps the most fun for the boys, because Dad would pretend he couldn't quite remember those names, then would ask the boys' opinions on what were some good puppy names, and whatever they came up with "just happened to be" the actual names of those puppies. There was always one named Little Queenie, but all the other names were up for grabs – Fuzzy, Prince, Mazie, Rex, Buddy, Skippy, and so on.

As stories go, the puppy story didn't have any real plot, and the "action" consisted solely of Queenie's bag of tricks, then the puppies playing with each other, wrasslin' and growlin' and rollin' around on the linoleum floor. But then came the good part, "the best part," where Grandma would fix them a special treat, mixing up a pan of crumbled-up corn bread, or "johnny cake," and warm milk, which she'd put down on the kitchen floor.

> *"An' all them puppies would gather round that pan, with their little tails all a-waggin' at once, an' they'd lick an' lick an' lick an' lick, until their little tummies were all just as tight as a drum, an' they'd licked that ol' pan just as clean as a whistle. An' then they'd commence to get sleepy, 'cause their bellies were so full an' they'd played so hard, so pretty soon they'd all start stretchin' an' a-yawnin', an' then one by one they'd waddle over and climb back into the box Grandma'd fixed up for Queenie an' them back behind the kitchen stove where it was warm, an' they'd turn themselves around a few times and then plop down an' snuggle up soft and tight against the ol' momma dog an' go sound asleep."*

That image, of sleeping puppies snuggled up tight against their momma, is undoubtedly the best ending ever invented for a bed-time story. No wonder my boys loved it. Later on, when my daughter Suzie was small, Dad and Mom lived too far away for us to see them very often, so it fell to me to tell her the puppy story, and it became her favorite way to fall asleep, with her daddy scratching her back and "telling about the puppies."

My folks provided me with a very stable and loving environment when I was a kid. I went through all twelve grades right here in Reed City and it was a wonderful place to grow up. My own kids weren't quite so lucky, especially my two boys. Jeff and Scott had attended four or five different schools by the time they graduated from high school – in Michigan, California, Germany and Maryland. So now when someone asks where they're from, they're never quite sure how to answer. Suzie was luckier. She was born in Germany, but did all her growing up in Maryland and went to school, K-12, with mostly the same crowd of kids, so she considers herself a Marylander, and even talks like one. She never had to cope with the myriad problems of being "the new kid," like her brothers did so many times. She has lived a couple years in Michigan now, and spent one year in Kentucky, but she wants to go back to Maryland, where she grew up. Maryland is home to her.

I think then that Suzie understands better than the boys why I came back to Reed City, after an absence of nearly thirty-five years. Because it's home. Because I missed it all those years, just as Suzie misses Maryland now. Jeff and Scott were not fortunate enough to have just one special place, one town that they could feel comfortable calling home. Scott, who lives in Pennsylvania, thinks of Michigan and Reed City as "the frozen north." Jeff, still in Maryland, has no particularly fond memories of the state where he was born, and I suspect he shares Scott's image of Michigan as a rather cold and inhospitable place to live.

Well, like me, my children have always enjoyed a good story. I can't line them all up on the couch anymore, with me in the middle to tell them a story, like we used to do. I wish I could, because I miss those days now. Instead (and I hope it's not too poor a substitute) I've written down a few stories and collected some memories to share with them. This book is a little like their grandpa's "puppy story," in that it doesn't have much of a plot, and hardly any real "action." But I'm hoping that, ultimately, it will leave them with a similar kind of warm feeling, and will also help to explain why I came back to where I started out so many years ago.

My dad has been gone for nearly fifteen years now, but I still miss him. I think he would have enjoyed these stories. My mom did when she read them. But I've finally written them down mostly for my kids: Jeff, Scott and Suzie. And I'm hoping that maybe some day their kids will read them too, and know who their grandpa was.

What follows is certainly not a comprehensive record of everything that happened to me when I was growing up, but it will have to do for now. I have tried to be as accurate and honest as possible, but most of these memories are from forty to fifty years ago, so there are bound to be some mistakes and inaccuracies, for which I apologize. I hope I don't offend or embarrass anyone, but here I am, warts and all – a Reed City boy.

Timothy James Bazzett
February 25, 2004
Reed City, Michigan

Geography and History

I'm a small town boy. I won't deny it. I spent twenty years living in the Baltimore-Washington corridor, but I never really felt at home there. I could never seem to get properly oriented there. I was never quite sure, even in my own neighborhood, exactly which way was north. So I'm starting this story – my story – in Reed City, my home town. If you're not from Michigan, you've probably never heard of Reed City. Heck, even if you've lived your whole life in Michigan, you could have missed it. So I'll put it on the map for you.

You've no doubt met someone from Michigan who, when you ask him where he's from in Michigan, will hold up his left hand, arm extended, fingers together, thumb apart. Then, pointing with his right hand, will show you where his particular town or village is located on the "mitten" that is Michigan's lower peninsula. Of course, if he happens to be from the upper peninsula, or the "UP," that's a whole different story. You'd need three hands to illustrate your location then. But "yoopers" *are* pretty strange. What with their small numbers, isolation, and

• Reed
• City

inbreeding, some of them might actually *have* three hands. (Just kidding, guys. Why, some of my best friends are yoopers.) So anyway, keeping this strange method of illustration in mind, if you are married, Reed City would be located exactly where your wedding band is worn. I have to confess that I got this particular explanation from my brother Bob, who, of course, also grew up in Reed City, and it is indeed the perfect way to pinpoint our little town on the mitten, right at the intersection of U.S. highways 131 and 10.

Approximately seventy miles south on 131 is Grand Rapids, once touted as the furniture capital of America, and the second most populous city in Michigan after Detroit. (I only just recently learned this fact, having assumed most of my life that our capital city, Lansing, was the state's second largest city.) Thirty miles north on 131 is Cadillac, the gateway to ski country. Forty-five miles to the west, on US 10, you'll come to Ludington, with its sandy beaches on the shores of Lake Michigan, where you can still catch a car ferry across the lake to Wisconsin. Equidistant to the east is Clare, but I can't think of anything to further distinguish that town, except perhaps as a way station south to Lansing, or further east to the tri-city area of Midland, Saginaw and Bay City, near Saginaw Bay and Lake Huron.

Why am I telling you all this? Well, I didn't want to do a *David Copperfield* kind of introduction to this thing, my story, if I actually do have a story to tell (which is what I'm trying to find out here). After all, everyone is, necessarily, the "hero" of his own story, but, for most ordinary people, it's difficult to think of oneself in heroic terms. Although my older son Jeff, when he was only five or six and his Grandma Zimmer asked him who was his hero, named me. Granted he was only five, but I've always remembered this, and, way in the back of my mind at least, have tried to live up to it. No, the reason I'm pinpointing precisely on the map where my story begins is that I have this thing, this idiosyncrasy if you will, of doing my reading with a road atlas (or sometimes a world atlas) close at hand so I can look up and verify the physical setting of a story or narrative. This may seem a little weird, but it works for me. I like to know the geography of what I'm reading.

I should probably clarify that, although I'm starting my story in Reed City, I was not born here. (Yeah, "here," because I'm back

Potterville, June 1944.
Rich holding baby Timmy.

Potterville, Spring 1945.
Left to Right:
Dad, Tim, Bob, Bill, Rich.

again, but that's getting way ahead of myself.) I was born in Charlotte, just southwest of Lansing (you can check your map now – no fictional settings here), at the Hayes-Green-Beech Hospital. I was the fourth of six children, which makes me kind of a middle child, but I don't have any of those typical "middle child" characteristics or problems (that would be my older brother Bob), because I was the "baby" for over seven years before my sister Mary was born, so I got plenty of love and attention for a long time. Mom was still rocking me when I was six and seven and big enough for my feet to reach the floor when I sat on her lap.

My dad was working at a grain elevator, or "mill," as elevators were still called back then, in Potterville (got your map?), and our family lived on a small "one-cow" farm just outside that little burg. I have absolutely no memories of Potterville, since we moved to Reed City when I was just over a year old. But my mom tells the story about when she brought me home from the hospital my three brothers all had the measles, or maybe it was the chicken pox, or maybe both in succession. (I really *must* become a better listener.) Anyway, I was kept in isolation and semi-darkness in my parents' bedroom, shades drawn, for the first couple months of my life. Maybe that's when I first acquired what was to become a life-long fondness for solitude and quiet. My kids will all tell you that when they were growing up and would ask me every year what I wanted for my birthday, I'd inevitably tell them, "A little peace and quiet."

My dad and mom. I probably should say something about them here. Where would I be without them, right? I wouldn't *be*. But this is *my* story, and I'm not sure how much of my folks' story I would get right, even though I've been hearing bits and pieces of it all my life. So I'll say a few things here, then hope that some of their story will emerge as I go along. I won't guarantee the accuracy of what I say about them, but here goes. Dad was the oldest of five boys. He was born in 1910 in Rockford, Michigan, to Julius and Mary Bazzett. They named him Ellis, my grandma's maiden name. By the time I got to know my grandpa "Judy," he was a tenant farmer on the old Steeby place just outside of Wayland, but he'd been other things too, including a logger and a city policeman in Grand Rapids. He still had a couple of his old billy clubs from that era and once showed my brothers and me the proper way for a cop to twirl his club, either with a strap attached, or without. We kids were pretty impressed. My Grandma "Mamie" had been a teacher briefly. She'd gotten a teaching certificate quite young. But back in those days, once you married, you didn't work at "outside" jobs. Marriage and motherhood was a full-time job, so she was always just "Grandma" to me, with her snow-white wavy hair and a kitchen that usually smelled of fresh-baked cookies.

Quite frankly, my dad's folks never had much, so Dad left home to find work as soon as he finished school. He was valedictorian at Wayland High School, class of 1927 (twenty-some students in his graduating class). He would no doubt have excelled in college, but he never figured that was even an option for him. There was no money to spare in the family and he needed to go to work and help out.

He worked at several small mills in Michigan, until he got hired at the *big* mill – General Mills – where he was a salesman for several years, peddling cereals, flour, cake mixes and other food products at various grocery stores and markets, first in the Detroit area, then for a time around Chicago. He was pretty good at it, but apparently never really liked it much, so was back to working in a

Ellis Edward Bazzett, valedictorian
Wayland High School, class of 1927.

Daisy Cecelia Whalen, valedictorian
Chesaning High School, class of 1932.

small town mill by the time I was born. I think probably Dad was always a small town boy at heart too, and never felt comfortable living in the city.

My mom was the third and youngest child of William and Lettie Whalen. She had two brothers, Harold and Clarence. Her folks named her Daisy, and she really is one. She was born in Oakley, Michigan, in 1916. Her dad, Will, was a rural mail carrier. Mom was always a pretty smart cookie. She loved to learn about everything and was a voracious reader. She must have impressed (or intimidated) some of her teachers, as she skipped a couple grades and finished high school before she was sixteen, graduating at the top of her class of twenty-seven students. Yup, Mom was a valedictorian too, Chesaning High School, class of 1932. Unlike Dad, however, she went on to college, where she continued to excel, and graduated near the top of her class at Central State Teachers College (now Central Michigan University) before she was twenty.

She taught English at Remus High School for just one year, before she married Dad. She had to keep their engagement a secret, or she probably wouldn't have gotten the job. Even by then, women just didn't work outside the home once they were married. But, unbeknownst to Dad, who was working in Detroit at the time, Mom

Dad with his 1930 Model A Ford Roadster ($525), 1933.

made the most of that one year of freedom after college, because, although she was engaged, she dated a few other men, mostly teachers, going to dances and picnics and other functions and generally having a good time, albeit with probably the teeniest twinges of guilt. She only told me about this recently and I was properly shocked. She said she kept these "dates" a secret from Dad until after they were married. Then, one night, feeling guilty about it all, she confessed her "profligacy" to him. She said Dad was terribly upset upon hearing of this, and wouldn't talk to her afterwards. It was summertime and at night when she told him. Dad walked out of the house and went out and lay down on the lawn and didn't come back in all night. The next morning he went off to work as usual and came home that night and acted as if she'd never told him anything, and the subject never came up again. This is Mom's version some sixty years later, so I'll have to accept it as fact, but I know my dad loved my mom deeply and was not above being jealous at the mere mention of any other man. There was plenty of love in our house when I was growing up, no question about it. We could feel it and we could see it between our folks. So Dad obviously "forgave" Mom, who was really only a twenty year-old girl having her first and last flings. They were married the day after she turned twenty-one. After that her family became her full-time job, for which I and my brothers and sister will always be thankful, because she was always there when we needed her, and was always our best teacher in all the things that are most important.

So that's my mom and dad, although obviously there will be more on them. And that's it for Potterville and Charlotte too, since, as I said, I don't remember anything about that first year or so of my life.

Dad inscribed this photo to Mom: "To the dearest girl I know. Love, Ellis." (March 3, 1936)

Ellis Bazzett and Daisy Whalen on their wedding day in Oakley, Michigan, June 26, 1937. Note the catalpa tree blossoms.

Reed City:
Holdenville and Early Memories

In 1945 my dad got an opportunity to go partners in a seed business and grain elevator in Reed City. I'd like to say that he jumped at the chance, but that probably wouldn't be strictly true. I don't think Dad ever "jumped" at anything. He always, in my memory anyway, carefully considered all the pros and cons of things, and only then made a decision. At any rate, he and his friend, Mick Churchill, bought the businesses, the Kent Elevator and the Churchill Seed Company, establishments that were to loom large in my growing-up years in Reed City.

Having bought into the business, Dad traveled north to Reed City alone and found a house for his rapidly growing family. It was located on the north end of town in a section called Holdenville. This is the first home that I remember. We lived there until 1952.

I need to say a few words about this house, and I had to ask my mom for some of these facts, which, although vague to me, are still clear in her mind over fifty years later. When Dad bought the house, there was some question as to whether it might be bug-infested, since the next-door neighbors, the Roggows, reported that they'd seen the previous occupants hauling their metal bedsprings outside and dousing them with boiling water before loading them up to move. So, just to be on the safe side, Dad closed up the house and lighted "bug bombs" in all the rooms to kill any unwanted

Kent Elevator in Reed City, June 1945.

Dad and his mill crew at the Kent Elevator, May 1949. L-R: Bernard Zeigler, Milt Steinhaus, Fay Zeigler, Ellis Bazzett.

pests, then went back to Potterville to collect his family and all their earthly possessions and bring them to our new home.

The house was a spacious one, according to Mom, but still pretty primitive, even by the standards of those times. There was no running water, hot *or* cold, in the house when we moved in, only a hand pump outside the back porch off the kitchen. That first year of occupancy, water had to be pumped into galvanized buckets and carried inside for washing up, for bathing, for drinking or cooking, for laundry, for *every*thing. If you wanted hot water, it had to be heated on the kitchen stove. There was no indoor toilet or bathroom, but an outhouse, or "privy," out back by the grapevine. (*Good* grapes off that vine.) The house had no furnace or central heating. There was an oil-burning heater in the living room to heat the main floor, with a ceiling grate to supply a meager amount of warmth to the bedroom above. Although an indoor bathroom and hot and cold running water were all installed within a year or two, the heating problem remained, and winters were *cold*!

The main floor of the house consisted of a long country kitchen, with a small enclosed back porch behind it. There's one thing I remember vividly about this unheated back porch. We kept a "slop pail" on the porch, where we emptied our peelings and

Holdenville house 1945.
Rich and Grandpa Whalen
putting plastic over windows.

garbage after meals, since this was well before the advent of under-the-sink garbage disposals. Every evening this slop pail was taken outside and emptied into a garbage pit, dug well away from the house, and then rinsed out and returned to the porch. This bucket also served another purpose. There were six of us living in this house (seven, after my sister Mary was born), and only one toilet. Bathroom traffic could be pretty heavy in the mornings, and when you gotta go, you gotta go. So, early on, Dad designated the slop pail as an emergency urinal, and it got used on a regular basis. Well, I'm here to tell you that there is no other sound in the world like that of a full bladder being emptied full-blast into an empty metal bucket on a frosty winter morning. BDDD-DDDD-DDDD-DDDD-TTTT!!! My brothers and I didn't enjoy the cold floor on our bare feet, but I think we all did kind of enjoy the impressive noise created by pissing into that bucket. Of course only the first pisser could enjoy that echoing rat-a-tat sound, so it was a race to the bucket in the morning. The winner got to make the noise while the rest of us waited, hopping anxiously from one foot to the other. The consolation prize was who could stir up the sudsiest yellow froth in subsequent pisses. The last one to use the bucket had to go empty it afterwards. Gee, the things we remember from our childhood.

Also on the main floor was a large living room. One of the focal points in that living room was a tall, floor model radio-phonograph, a Zenith, I think, but I could be wrong. It was the big

Holdenville, fall 1946. L-R: Tim, Bob, Bill, Rich.
From special feature "Meet Reed City's Children" in Osceola Herald.

heavy kind with vacuum tubes, that took a minute or two to warm up. It had an ornately carved front with a cloth-covered speaker. We got a lot of miles out of that old radio. (Later it was re-located to our summer cottage and stayed in use for a long time.) On weekdays after school, I used to sit in front of that radio and listen to shows like, "The Cinnamon Bear," "Let's Pretend," "The Adventures of Mark Trail," and "Clyde Beatty's Circus." Saturday mornings we listened to "Bobby Benson and the B-Bar-B Ranch." But Sunday nights held the best radio family fare, starting with "Gene Autry's Melody Ranch." Later you could hear Jack Benny, Bing Crosby, and shows like "Amos and Andy," "My Little Margie," or "The Lone Ranger." Every Sunday night our whole family would gather at the radio, Mom and Dad on the couch and we kids sitting on the floor right in front of the speaker, all of us with bowls of popcorn to "watch radio." The pictures were all in your mind, and you were never disappointed. Imagination was all.

Where was I? Oh, yeah. All those radio adventures were in the living room. Just off that room, there was an equally roomy "parlour," which became the kids' bedroom, holding a double bed and two single beds. My older brothers, Rich and Bill, slept in the single beds. Bob and I, as the two youngest boys, shared the double bed. I keep thinking of Bill Cosby's hilarious album, *My Brother Russel, Whom I Slept With,* and all the funny anecdotes that came out of his experience, but I just can't seem to come up with any funny stuff about Bob and I sharing a bed, except that I probably wet that bed a few times, which Bob probably didn't find very funny.

11

Mary Jane Bazzett, Mom's only girl, born in Holdenville on May 20, 1951.
L-R: Bob, Tim, Rich, Mary, Bill.

There was an archway opening off this parlour-dormitory room into a small alcove that had once been a "music room." Mom and dad's bed was in there, separated from us only by a heavy curtain. This arrangement certainly couldn't have afforded them much privacy, but I guess there must have been *some,* since my sister Mary was born in 1951 (after a brother, Tommy, stillborn in 1949).

Upstairs there were four big bedrooms, all pretty cold in the winter, but when Rich and Bill got a little older, they relocated to the bedroom over the living room, where the ceiling grate provided them with minimal warmth. I can remember them though, on frigid winter mornings, hustling down the stairs still in their pajamas to get dressed next to the stove in the living room. In the biggest unused bedroom, over the kitchen, Mom stretched clotheslines and hung laundry to dry there in the wintertime and on rainy days – no electric or gas dryers back then either; everything got hung up on clotheslines. One of the jobs we kids helped out with whenever Mom could corral us was hanging up and taking down the wash from the outside clotheslines. When I was little I handed Mom the clothespins, but as I got taller I could help her take down the sheets and fold them into the basket, or sometimes I would carry the trousers that were made awkward by the pants stretchers that were inserted into the legs to make them dry flat and less wrinkled and twisted.

There was also a wide front porch off the parlour-bedroom that overlooked a small field and John Stager's farmhouse to the south. One of my earliest memories of Holdenville is walking in the damp dark furrows of earth that were turned over in that field when Charlie Ripley came in with his team of work horses to help John with the plowing one Spring. (This scene was preserved for posterity on one of our home movies too.) To me those horses seemed impossibly enormous as I walked along beside and behind them, watching them plod placidly ahead of the plow. Bob and I would follow along in each fresh furrow with a tin can for gathering up earthworms that surfaced, so Dad would have bait for fishing on Sundays, and every now and then we'd find some other treasure too, like an Indian arrowhead or stone axe head.

Our house was located on the west side of Roth Street, which ran north-south all the way through town. Although we were kind of out in the country, we were also within walking distance to downtown, and we used to walk to the movies from there on Saturday afternoons, along with other kids who lived nearby – Kenny Roggow, the Rohe boys, and sometimes Roger and Violet Stager.

My memories of the Holdenville house are somewhat fragmented and vague, but they are mostly good, happy ones. Maybe that's because we tend to repress the bad memories, but I prefer to think that I just had a happy childhood.

My very earliest memory sounds kind of silly and insignificant, but it is a warm and fuzzy one if ever there was one, so I'll mention it. I was probably only three or four, and I remember Mom putting me down on my bed and tucking me in for my nap, along with a favorite toy, a pink oil-cloth covered *Bambi*. (Walt Disney's animated film was only a couple years old then.) There was something literally "warm and fuzzy" about this experience, since a nap meant you slept on *top* of the bedclothes and covered up with an Army blanket. We had several of these WWII surplus blankets, which were brown and fuzzy, and usually folded at the foots of our beds for cold nights – or to cover up with while napping. After Mom tucked me in, she'd usually go into the living room and run the vacuum cleaner, a soothing, regular sound that never failed to put me promptly to sleep. And to this day, the sound of a vacuum cleaner running in another room makes me feel safe – and sleepy.

In contrast to this pleasant memory, there were, of course, some unpleasant, even traumatic things that happened to me in those first years in the Holdenville house, things I don't remember, but have been told to me often enough that they have become "shadow memories." One was a kitchen accident that could have been disfiguring, but thanks to Mom's TLC and quick action, was not. It happened when I was about two, and, in trying to climb up onto a kitchen counter to look out the window, I upended a can of hot bacon grease onto my hand and arm. According to Mom, we *both* cried for much of the day afterwards, as she carried me all around the house and yard trying to comfort me – this *after* she had applied whatever first aid was available, probably cold water and butter. Afterwards she sewed a small cotton sack to keep my hand covered, salved and protected while it healed. Her instinctive ministrations must have worked, because I bear no scars from this incident.

Another later episode, however, did leave me with a physical scar, in addition to leaving my poor mother with yet another traumatizing memory. I was about three when my brother Bob and I were playing in the yard one day and Bob was practicing his rock-throwing skills. He decided to try to throw a rock over the roof of the house (pretty ambitious for a four or five year-old kid). I must have been pretty impressed by his skills though, because I was standing right in front of him watching his wind-up. Well, his throw fell considerably short of its expressed goal, and I took the rock squarely in the center of my forehead. There was, apparently, an immediate and dramatic abundance of blood, as is usually the case with any kind of head wound, even a superficial one, which this was. I instantly started bawling like a banshee from the pain and shock, and Bob, seeing the blood and hearing my screams, was set off too, bringing Mom on the run out of the kitchen. I can only imagine what she must have felt, seeing her baby screaming, face and shirt already covered with blood, and Bob wailing too. Poor Mom. Of course, once she got me cleaned up she could see it was only a small cut, so she staunched the bleeding and bandaged it and that was that, although I still have a small crescent-shaped scar as a reminder – of an event I don't actually remember myself. See? The bad memories *do* get repressed – and that's probably a good thing.

Tim and Bob, circa 1947.
Uneasy roommates and
playmates for over eighteen years.

Bill and Tim in Holdenville 1946.
Bill should have been my roommate.
Our temperaments were more similar.

Here's another rather unpleasant early memory, and this one I *do* remember personally. It involved a tricycle and, again, my brother Bob – hmmm. I guess I might as well mention here that Bob and I *never* got along very well, although we were thrust together as uneasy playmates – and roommates – for eighteen years. Looking back at those living arrangements, it's easy to see in hindsight that Bill and I would have made more suitable roommates, and Rich and Bob probably would have gotten along well too – certainly better that Bob and I ever did. But we were billeted by order of birth in those days, as were most kids in big families, so Bob and I were stuck with each other. Bob exhibited certain unhappy and aggressive elements of the "middle child" syndrome, squeezed between Bill and me with less than a year and a half separating him on either side. He probably never got enough cuddling. In temperament Bob and I were always complete opposites. He was an aggressive, ambitious, can-do go-getter type (and still is). I was always more tentative, shy, perhaps a bit fearful of things, something of a dreamer. As the younger brother, I was easy to take advantage of – an easy mark. The concept of sharing never came easily to Bob, and therein lies the tale of the tricycle.

I was probably around four or five when Mom and Dad unearthed an old tricycle that had been Rich and Bill's previously and had been packed away for a time after the move to Reed City. In presenting us with the trike, Mom instructed us firmly that we were to "take turns" with it. Well, in the excitement of pedaling maniacally about on this "new" vehicle, it was easy to forget about the sharing part, so our "turns" in the saddle quickly became quite unequal, with Bob pointedly abusing his superior older brother status. Mom, forced into the role of arbitrator, brought out a kitchen timer, which she placed on the porch and set for five minutes, explaining that when the timer dinged whoever was riding should surrender the saddle. This way we would each have equal turns on the trike. We agreed to this arrangement, and Bob, of course, took the first turn.

Those five minutes seemed like an eternity to me, as Bob, a superior smirk on his lips, maneuvered smoothly up and down the

Tim and Bob and little red wagon, circa 1948. Bob was always pushing me around.

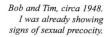

Bob and Tim, circa 1948. I was already showing signs of sexual precocity.

sidewalk that ran from our side porch down to Roth Street, where several cement steps descended to the ditch along the road. The timer finally dinged just as he was reaching the porch for the umpteenth time, but instead of turning the trike over to me, he wheeled quickly around in a tight circle and sped back down the walk, his shoulders hunched in concentration over the handlebars, his feet rotating furiously, with me in hot pursuit, crying, "No fair! It's *MY TURN!*" Sneaking a sneering look back over his tee-shirted shoulder, Bob momentarily forgot how short the sidewalk actually was, and went plunging down the concrete steps, tricycle and all, into the ditch, a tangled welter of metal handlebars and spokes, rubber wheels and skinny knees and elbows. More blood, more screaming, more trauma. Poor Mom.

Question: If this is a *bad* memory, how come I remember it? What happened to that usually reliable repression theory? Maybe I remember it because it was more of a bad memory for Bob than it was for me? I'd like to think of it as an early experience of "good" (me) triumphing over "evil" (Bob), but I can't quite manage it. After all, you're always going to be the "good guy" in your own story. If this were Bob's story, he'd probably be remembering what a stupid pest and crybaby I was as his little brother.

Singing Cowboys
and Saturday Matinees

"Good guys" played a major role in our games in the late forties and early fifties. Two of the biggest box office stars of that time were the singing cowboys Gene Autry and Roy Rogers. In their heyday, their popularity matched or surpassed that of classic matinee idols like Clark Gable and Gary Cooper, stars I didn't come to appreciate until I was considerably older. Saturday afternoon was the high point of my week as a kid, as it was for many kids throughout the country. On Saturdays the B-western reigned supreme at the the kiddie matinees. Gene and Roy were the best, of course, but there were other, lesser stars that were equally acceptable.

There was Johnny Mack Brown, whose specialty was the barroom fist fight, which he never started, but always won, after which he would meticulously pick up his hat, dust it off and re-seat it carefully on his head, pull up his leather riding gloves and hitch up his cartridge belt. Then he would step calmly up to the bar and order a "sarsaparilla, please." (For you tenderfoots, that's a "sody pop.") Unfailingly polite, champion brawler, Johnny Mack was always a gentleman. (He *did* tend to bounce a bit too much in the saddle during the chase scenes though.)

"Wild Bill" Elliott's special "draw" was the way he wore his twin six-guns, with holsters backwards, gun butts facing forward.

When he executed his quick draw – and he *was fast* – he reached across his body with both hands and whipped those pistols out in a broad flamboyant arc, both barrels blazing – a move we practiced often in our games at home, but could never quite do it the way Wild Bill did it. By the way, Wild Bill always ordered milk at the bar, which would inevitably cause some swarthy baddie to ridicule him, leading to – you guessed it – a barroom brawl.

Lash LaRue, dressed all in black, was another rare favorite, whose weapon of choice in a faceoff was a wicked-looking bullwhip he wore coiled at his belt. It seems hard to believe, in retrospect, that anyone could draw, uncoil and strike out with a whip faster than the "bad guy" could draw his gun, but ol' Lash could do it, by golly. At the age of eight or nine, employing Coleridge's "willing suspension of disbelief" principle was no problem, especially when the good guy wins. (Coleridge? Who's *Col*eridge?)

There were numerous other stars of this genre: Rex Allen, Jimmy Wakely, Sunset Carson, Don "Red" Barry (aka *Red Ryder*), the Durango Kid, Tim Holt, Bob Steele and the Three Mesquiteers. Even the Duke himself, John Wayne, was featured in a few one-reel oaters as "Singin' Sandy," with his songs overdubbed by an anonymous Nelson Eddy sound-alike. (Sorry, Duke, but those films were *really* lame.)

But there was never any doubt that Gene and Roy were the best. Gene Autry was always my favorite of the two, maybe because he was just a little less flashy, and maybe, just a teensy bit, because he reminded me of my dad. Roy was this little, wiry athletic guy with the squinty, almost Chinese-looking eyes who took pride in doing most of his own stunts. He wore fancy, colorful, western-style snap-button fringed shirts and tight form-fitting striped trousers tucked into elaborately hand-tooled high-heeled boots, topped off with a snowy white stetson. Gene, on the other hand, although he sometimes sported the fancy duds, would, often as not, be attired in an ordinary shirt and dungarees worn with turned-up bottoms over plain brown boots. But he *did* wear a white stetson. Good guys almost always wore white hats. (Well, except for Lash and the Durango Kid, but their black hats were necessary to complete their all-black ensembles.) Gene never seemed the athletic type either, and even got a little fat later in his movie career,

Holdenville cowboys, circa 1948. L-R: Bill, Tim, Bob, Kenny Roggow.
Note everyone else in full cowboy regalia, vests, chaps and all, while I'm in hand-me-downs.
And what's with that sock for a holster?

after the war, almost certainly a victim of creeping Dunlop's Disorder. (That's when your belly dunlops over your belt.)

Their horses were important parts of their image too. Gene had Champion, or "Champ, " a beautiful chestnut stallion with a flowing blonde mane and tail, that not only appeared in all Gene's feature films, but also accompanied him on tour around the countryside. Dad once took us to see Gene and his entourage when he made an appearance at the Civic Auditorium in Grand Rapids. Champ was there too, and Gene put him through his paces, then brought out "Little Champ," Champion's colt, who also performed a few simple tricks. It was a truly memorable night for us front row kids from Reed City.

Roy, of course, had Trigger, his beautiful Palomino, always billed as the "smartest horse in the movies." Gene could have taken issue with this, I suppose, but never did. Rex Allen had his Koko, the Lone Ranger had Silver, and Tonto his Scout. Even back in the silent film era, Tom Mix had his Tony.

And then there was the music. There were other "singing cowboys" around at the time. Rex Allen had a pleasant baritone; Jimmy Wakely sounded uncannily *like* Gene Autry; and Tex Ritter had a pretty authentic cowboy sound. But there was really nobody with the style and sound of Gene and Roy. I loved the musical interludes in their movies almost as much as the shoot-em-up action scenes. My mom remembers how, when my brothers and I would return from a Gene Autry matinee on Saturday afternoons, all four of us would sit in a row on the sofa, and, rocking rhythmically from the waist, doing our best to simulate the easy motion of a cowboy in the saddle, we would all sing: "I'm backin ya saddo a-gaainn." Yeah, we revered Gene and Roy in those days. I still love their music and own boxed CD sets of their best songs.

Like Willie Nelson's song says, "My Heroes Have Always Been Cowboys," and this dates back to those much anticipated Saturday matinees at the Reed Theater in the nineteen-fifties. Every Saturday Mom would give each of us – Rich, Bill, Bob and me – fifty cents to spend. It was a little less than a mile walk into town. The box office opened at 11:30 and curtain time was noon. The price of admission was twelve cents for kids under twelve. Adults and kids over twelve had to pay a quarter. A bag of popcorn was a dime, candy cost a nickel. So, after paying admission and having popcorn and candy to go with the movies, we still had money left over to go to Bonsall's or Dykstra's drug store afterwards and buy a comic book (a dime) and a Coke (five or ten cents). And then we *still* had a few cents left over to hoard until next week or to buy

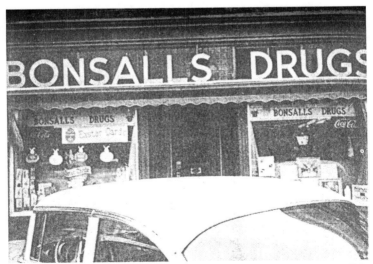

Bonsall's Drugs on West Upton, 1961.

21

penny candy at the Ben Franklin or Starr's Five and Dime during the week. Such a deal! Life was indeed good at that age.

Those afternoon matinees really were a great deal too, for everyone concerned. Theater owner Norris Stafford would fill his place to capacity every Saturday, while keeping most of the kids in town out of their parents' hair for three hours or so. The show would open with cartoons – Tom and Jerry, Mighty Mouse, The Terry Bears, Droopy, Mickey Mouse or Bugs Bunny – sometimes two or three in succession if there was a "cartoon carnival." Then would come the serial, a segmented feature continued from one week to the next, *always* with a "cliff-hanger" (often literally) ending. These could be westerns (one of Gene Autry's first films was a serialized "sci-fi western" called *The Phantom Empire*), Superman or Batman tales, or "G-men" (government agents) spy stories. Then the feature film, or, often as not, a double feature would follow, inevitably a comedy and a western. The comedies usually featured the Bowery Boys (aka the East End Kids), with Leo Gorcey and Huntz Hall as "Slip Mahoney" and "Satch," respectively. Or it could be the Little Rascals, with Spanky, Alfalfa, Buckwheat, Darla and company. The western was usually served up last.

So it would often be 3:00 or later by the time we emerged from the darkened theater, blinking and squinting in the sudden daylight, to make our foray to the drug store, where I often ended up buying the latest issue of Gene's or Roy's comic book and slurping down a cherry Coke. Then we'd be on our way back home, galloping on our imaginary mounts around the corner of Upton and north up Chestnut, over the bridge spanning the Hersey River, across US 10, and up the hill to our house, where Mom would be getting ready for Saturday supper, usually hamburgers and ice cream, one of our favorite meals. That evening we would all lie sprawled on the living room floor reading and trading our new comics, a perfect end to a perfect day.

This steady diet of B-western movies did, of course, influence our games and play too. We "played cowboys" a lot in those days. Our games were ninety-eight percent imagination and two per cent props. We did have an assortment of western-style cap-guns, a few holsters and hats, and we could always find a big blue or red patterned handkerchief to roll up and tie around our necks for

*Timmy "Tex" Bazzett, 1950.
"You better smile when you say that,
hombre."*

*The "Holdenville-in-the-Wall Gang," 1950. New hats all around. L-R: Rich, Bob, Kenny
Roggow, Roger Stager (in aviator cap), Tim, Bill. Note Rich and Bill's "hightop" shoes.*

"bandanas." Hats, or "sombreros" (if we happened to be playing
Cisco Kid and Pancho) were always important accessories. I
remember one year for my birthday I asked my folks for not just *a*
cowboy hat for myself, but for hats for *all* of us – for Rich, Bill,
Bob and me – so we could all be properly outfitted at once, I
suppose – and we *got* them too! That was a really great birthday.

The hats themselves weren't much, thin little white, red or black felt contrivances with perhaps a bit of contrasting trim, but they made an immense difference in our games, and we often spent an inordinate amount of time trying to block and crease our hats just so, the way Red Ryder or Lash LaRue wore their hats.

During those long idyllic days of Holdenville summers we would spend hours making up stories and scenarios, then staging our own little adventures of ambushes, stage robberies, stampedes and hair-raising Pony Express rides through hostile Indian country of the nearby sandpits, or bellying up to imaginary or makeshift bars and manfully ordering a "shot of redeye, barkeep." (Or, if you were Wild Bill Elliot, a "glass of milk," which would always somehow precipitate that bust-em-up fist fight.)

Of course, we had no horses for these games, but we never noticed that. "Simulated riding" came naturally to all of us, a kind of stutter-step gait we easily assumed, accompanied by vocal sound effects which varied in pitch and sound, depending on whether we were walking, trotting, cantering or galloping our mounts. Bill was the best at these sound effects and also at coming up with plot-lines and realistically acting out our scenarios. Once, as a result of striving for such authenticity, he was demonstrating the fine art of pistol-whipping (something only a "bad guy" would do), and accidentally whacked me full in the mouth (I turned my head at the wrong time) with the butt of his cap pistol, chipping a corner off a front tooth. I still have that minute gap in my smile – a reminder of my cowboy days.

War Games, Comics
and Stuffed Toy Bunnies

The other game we played at often was "war," as in, "Let's play war today, instead of cowboys." This was natural enough at the time. The Korean War was in progress and then winding down, and World War II was still a fairly fresh wound in the the collective memory of America. Hollywood was churning out war movies by the dozen, with stars like John Wayne, Gary Cooper, Alan Ladd, Robert Mitchum, and – our personal favorite – Audie Murphy, a genuine war hero turned actor. Murphy penned his own story, *To Hell and Back*, then played himself in the film version, a story of front-line heroism that captured the imagination of kids everywhere. Murphy was a natural for kids to emulate too, due to his diminutive stature and boyish looks. (Interestingly, the bulk of Murphy's subsequent films, in a less than stellar acting career, were westerns. The best of these was John Huston's *The Unforgiven*, in which Murphy effectively co-starred with Burt Lancaster and Audrey Hepburn.)

Our next-door neighbor, Kenny Roggow, had a bunch of army clothes, hats, caps and helmets, handed down from his much older brother, Bud, a war veteran. My brothers and I shared a few hats and a helmet liner we'd somehow gotten from our Uncle Vern, who'd served in Both WWII and Korea. My oldest brother, Rich, who was soon to forsake us as playmates and spend much of his time outside school working at the elevator with Dad, helped to "arm" us all for our war games. Dad had recently purchased a jigsaw and set it up in the garage, although I'm not sure Dad himself ever used it much. (Dad never was very handy with tools, a trait that most of his kids inherited.) Rich did teach himself how to use the saw though, and, drawing outlines on scrap pieces of boards or plywood, he cut us out a dozen or more mock weapons – pistols, rifles, bayonets, and, best of all, "tommy guns," with the two signature grips and the multi-round magazine, which you could fire practically forever and never be accused of "running out of ammo."

The perfect venue for our imaginary conflicts was the little sandpit, located between our place and Roggow's. There we dug trenches and foxholes and built elaborate "pill boxes" and bunkers, digging with hands and sticks, and covering over our deep holes with old boards, brush, and sand, then hunkering down inside them, sometimes popping out to take potshots or lob crab apple "grenades" at imaginary Nazis or "Japs" (no political correctness in our terminology back then, sorry). It's surprising, looking back, that none of these holes caved in on us and killed us. But probably no more surprising than the fact that we didn't sustain any broken arms or legs when we used to jump off Kenny Roggow's garage roof, playing paratroopers. The only real injury I can remember from these games was when Bob once stepped on an old board with a rusty nail sticking out of it and the nail went right through his sneakered foot. I'm sure the healing powers of Mom were once again invoked, but I can't remember if a doctor visit or tetanus shot was called for.

Such was the stuff of our playtime when the weather was good and the sun shone. On rainy days, however, we would bring stacks of old comic books and congregate in Roggow's garage and lie on the floor and trade comics and read and share the best parts from the adventures of Captain Marvel, Batman, Aquaman, Plastic Man, Red Ryder and Little Beaver, Hoppy, Gene and Roy, of course, and – one of my personal favorites – Walt Disney's Uncle Scrooge McDuck (Donald Duck's uncle). Scrooge was a zillionaire tightwad who kept all his money in a multi-storied "money bin" so he could dive into it and roll in it and swim around in it, a concept that, for some unfathomable reason, appealed to us kids. He was constantly besieged by a notorious gang of ex-cons called the Beagle Boys, who thought up ingenious schemes to relieve Scrooge of his millions. Donald and his three nephews, Huey, Dewey and Louie, always played prominent roles in the stories, which often incorporated rather literary plot lines based on classics, like *King Solomon's Mines* or the children's fairy tale, *King of the Golden River*. Scrooge comics were, in short, something special, and worth collecting and reading over and over again.

Superman was also a perennial favorite, and a hero we often tried to emulate. Roggow's garage roof came in handy again in this respect. We once spent most of a drizzly summer afternoon taking turns jumping off that roof, an old pink towel strung around our neck, dramatically declaiming, "Up, up and a-waaaay!" – the closest we could come to flying. (Don't tell Mom, OK?)

Another guilty-pleasure indoor activity for Bill, Bob and me was playing with our stuffed bunnies. Now I know that sounds pretty sissy – probably why I *now* call it a "guilty pleasure" – but I don't think we ever felt that way about it at the time. You have to bear in mind that there weren't that many action figure sorts of toys available at that time, and we probably couldn't afford those that were around. So Mom had sewed us each a small bunny, a homemade equivalent of a jointed, action figure, with arms and legs that were fastened onto the head-torso with heavy-duty thread so you could move them up and down and position them. (Of course, sometimes these limbs would come off, but Mom would just take a minute and sew them back on for us.)

One of the older bunnies

Each of these bunnies had given names (given by *whom,* I'm not sure). Bill's bunny (which I think was originally Rich's) was Thumper (probably named after the rabbit in Disney's *Bambi*), and was a rather non-descript gray color, due to its advanced age and countless handlings, and had been patched numerous times. Bob's bunny was a dirty pink one named Bunny Belle (smirk, smirk). Mine was blue and was called Honey Bunny (oh, well). Thumper was always Thumper, but Bob and I re-named ours, of course. Bunny Belle became Charley, and Honey Bunny morphed into Marty.

These bunnies were our poor kids nineteen-fifties equivalent of what my own kids always called all their action figures – "little rubber guys." We used another homemade unidentifiable stuffed animal called Brownie as a horse for our bunnies when they were cowboys. We built covered wagons for them out of shoe boxes, Tinker-Toy wheels, wire coat hangers and handkerchiefs. For more modern scenarios, we fashioned airplanes out of Morton salt boxes by cutting a cockpit opening in one side and a slot underneath it to slide a cardboard wing-piece through, which the bunny pilot also used as a seat. Aerial dog-fights were fought throughout the skies of our bedrooms by these bunny-piloted Sopwith Camels, Messerschmidts, and Sabre Jets. Imagination was obviously key in our games, something which seems lost with todays toys that all have to "do something" and require only batteries – no imagination.

A later generation of homemade stuffed bunnies.

Winter Fun
or "Blood on the Snow"

The often bitterly cold winters of Michigan were not an obstacle to outdoor play for us. The roads around town became snowpacked and hard as iron after several snowfalls and repeated plowing. Then, after a slight thaw and subsequent freeze, these roads became perfect for sliding. We all had sleds, the old "flexible flier" kind you rarely see anymore, as they have been largely replaced by toboggans and snowboards. Our sleds had steel runners and wood-slatted bodies with a steering bar at the front end. There were two ways to ride these sleds. The "safe" way, or little kid way, was to sit on the sled, using your feet to operate the steering bar. The more dangerous way, and certainly the much preferred one, was to make a running start while carrying the sled at chest level, then fling yourself down, belly-flopping onto the sled, head up, steering with your hands. You could fly faster this way (less wind resistance) and go farther down the hill. Of course, there were no helmets or pads for any of this back then. Danger or injury never entered our minds. The thrill was the thing, and skill was important.

When we lived in Holdenville, our most common sledding site was Roth Street, which conveniently had the crest of a good hill right next to our house. Yes, we did most of our sledding right in the roadway, traffic dangers be damned. And, at the bottom of our block, if the road was icy enough and the momentum could be

Holdenville house, 1951. Tim with his trusty "flexible flier" sled. Note new front porch.

maintained, we could even make it across a major highway, US 10, just past John Stager's barn. If you saw traffic approaching, you could always wipe out into the big sandpit on the west side of Roth. At least that was how it would work in theory. I can't remember anyone ever being hit by a car, so I guess we were pretty lucky.

Another favorite hill, famous to all the kids in town, was Pease's Hill, about a mile or so up the road northeast of our house. We used to trek that distance, bundled up in our heavy coats, scarves and mittens, winter caps with earflaps down, and rubber four-buckle arctic boots, pulling our sleds behind us. Pease's Hill was on a road too, but a less-traveled back road. It boasted an initially steep crest, then a long gradual slope of what seemed like a mile or more, flattening out near the end at a narrow, one-lane bridge over a creek. The aim in sledding Pease's Hill was to make it all the way across that bridge, but you needed extremely icy conditions to achieve that goal. And it was a long walk back to the top of the hill, but we did it over and over again, using that time to discuss the finer points of the takeoff run, the perfect belly-flop, or the best way to pump your feet and legs near the end of the run to achieve maximum distance. We must have walked and sledded for miles and miles on those frigid winter days, and loved every minute of it, dragging ourselves home afterwards to consume enormous hot meals and then falling exhausted into our beds to sleep.

Although, as I said, I can't remember any fatal sledding accidents, there were occasional accidents, and I had a pretty serious one myself, a few years after we had moved across town to West Church Avenue. I had just turned twelve, and, along with a neighbor kid, Ned Seath, was out after school looking for a new hill to conquer. The south end of town had fewer classic sledding hills than the north side, so we were always on the lookout for a challenge. There had been an ice storm a day or two earlier, so most of the streets and hillsides were still a blinding glare of ice, making sledding extremely dangerous, since your steering rudder was practically useless under such conditions. (*Now* I know that; I didn't *then*.) But it was a bright sunny day, with temperatures hovering around zero, and Ned and I were ready for some chills and thrills.

The Holdenville olympic bobsled team, circa 1951.
L-R: Rich, Bill, Bob, Tim, Roger Stager, Kenny Roggow (and his dog, Bomber).

31

We selected the crest of a hill behind old Mr. Parish's house , about a half a block from home. It looked promising. The launching point was very steep, probably a near forty-five degree grade, then halfway down the hill, we needed to make a sharp turn to the right, in order to end up coming down a slope between McDowell's and Wood's houses. If you missed that turn, you'd plunge over an embankment about 15 feet high into a small field between the houses. Undaunted by the dangerous conditions, we pushed off. Ned went first. He made the turn. I did not.

I went over the edge of the bank. Hidden just below the snow-covered lip of the embankment was a steel surveyor's stake, protruding several inches out of the ice and snow. As I slewed out of control over this small cliff, desperately trying to turn, my lower body came off the sled and the jagged edge of the stake caught me high on the inside of my left thigh, tearing through my pants and laying open my leg almost to the knee. I was probably already in shock as I tumbled and rolled, along with my sled, down the embankment, finally coming to rest near the middle of the field. I don't remember actually feeling any pain, but when I looked down at my leg and saw it lying open to the sun and sky, blood pooling around it, I instinctively reached down with both hands and gathered the two sides of the gaping wound together the best I could. I must have already been screaming, probably more from terror than pain, because Ned came running, eyes wide with fear and wonder, not just at the sight of my injury, I later found out, but at the scarlet, blood-spattered trail I'd left behind me, from the top of the bank all the way down to where I now lay. Panicked, he ran for help, never thinking of going to the first house, but instead running all the way back to my house to tell my mom, who immediately phoned Dad at the elevator. Dad must have called the ambulance before jumping in his car and speeding the several blocks through town to the field where he found me, lying in shock. Years later, Dad told me that when he saw the blood-smeared trail in that bright snow field, with me at the end of it, he nearly fainted, certain that I would die. But he came rushing to my side, his face white, and did what he could to calm and comfort me, pulling his big red work handkerchief out of his pocket and laying it gently over my injured leg, which I was still holding together with both hands. I don't know how long I lay in that field, probably no more

Clipping of sledding accident from the Osceola Herald, February 2, 1956.

1951 – Holdenville: Tim

than twenty minutes, until the ambulance arrived. I think my mind kind of shut down out of shock, and time stood still, at least until Dad arrived, and then I knew everything would be all right, because my dad said it would be.

In remembering this, and finally writing it all down, I am moved to tears, because, perhaps for the first time, I can now feel my father's fear and pain at witnessing such a gory accident scene involving one of his kids. (I can also understand why his hair turned white at an early age.) But Dad kept his cool and did what he had to do. By the time I was loaded into the ambulance, Dad must have been reassured that my life wasn't in any immediate danger. I remember him sitting beside me in the ambulance as we sirened the few short blocks to the hospital and musing, "You know, this is the first time I've ever been inside an ambulance." Calmer myself by then, I thought , *Me too, Dad.*

The wound initially took about 25 stitches to close, but because of the ragged edges and uneven shape, it didn't heal properly. Some of the skin actually began to turn gray and rot, so,

1951 – Holdenville: Mary, Dad and Rich, Bob, Tim and Bill

weeks later, the wound was re-opened, the edges were pulled snug, and it was stitched up again by Dr. Kilmer, this time requiring 32 stitches. This time it did heal, but very slowly, finally leaving me with a long crooked flattened pink scar, nearly ten inches long. The accident happened at the end of January, and I was still wearing a dressing and bandage in July. I missed the rest of that school year (but did schoolwork at home, so stayed with my class) and a whole summer of swimming because of that one stupid stunt. I was hospitalized for weeks and couldn't walk for months. Mom brought our Radio Flyer red wagon into the house when I got home and I used it to scoot around downstairs, pushing with my good leg. I went up and down the stairs on my butt. I got to know many of Mom's favorite radio shows during my lengthy convalescence at home, like *Don McNeil's Breakfast Club* and *The Arthur Godfrey Show*, but it was still a frustratingly long and slow recovery.

So, yes, Virginia, sledding *can* be dangerous. I never did much sledding again after that, as I was into my teenage years by then, and interested in other things. But I'm not ready yet to "put away childish things." I've gotten ahead of myself in the name of smooth transitions, something Sister Justin always taught me was important in good writing.

Indian Lake

In 1951 my dad must have begun feeling somewhat secure in his new business, and perhaps even a bit prosperous, because that was the year he had a cabin built on the north end of Indian Lake. This cabin opened up a whole new level of summer fun for my brothers and me, and, later on, for my sister Mary, who was born that same year. Dad hired Matt Matzella, a general contractor with a good reputation, who, along with his numerous sons, built many homes and cottages in and around Reed City. The foundation was laid and the construction began in the spring and continued through that summer. Every Sunday Mom and Dad would pack us all into the car, along with a picnic lunch, and we'd travel the twelve miles north and east to the lake where we would swim and feast, and we boys would clamber about in the crawl space under the cabin and, later, all over the gradually growing house. The cabin had varnished log siding on the outside and knotty pine paneling on the inside. There was a sleeping loft in the west half of the cabin where all of us kids slept once it was completed. Downstairs under the loft was a private bedroom for Mom and Dad. The rest of the downstairs was an open "great room" with kitchen, living and dining areas. Our dining room table was a heavy, varnished pine picnic table with attached benches. Dad and Mom sat in chairs at either end during meals and we kids filled up the benches on both sides. In the kitchen was a propane gas cookstove, a refrigerator

Our new cabin on Indian Lake, 1951.

and a hand-operated pump mounted at the end of a counter over the sink. A fireplace was centered on the east wall, and we often built fires in it on chilly spring and summer evenings. There was no ceiling in the great room, just the rafters between the living space and the roof. The temptation was great for us kids to hang out over the loft railing and throw things up and down, but this was much frowned upon by the management.

The toilet was a two-holer in an outhouse about thirty feet out from the back door. A bath or shower was, of course, unnecessary. We had a whole lake right out front. All you needed was a bar of the soap that floats – Ivory.

There was a wide screened-in front porch that extended across the whole front of the house, facing the lake. Many a rainy summer day was spent on that porch, playing board games or a guessing game ("I'm thinking of something ..."), and waiting impatiently for the sun to come out so we could get back into the water again. There was always a hammock on that porch, a much-contested place to lie during daytime games and also as a sleeping spot at night.

We were surrounded by other kids at the lake, from other cottages along the north and east sides of the lake. (The south end was a kind of public beach, and the west side of the lake was mostly a pasture where you could sometimes see cows come down to the lake to drink or stand in the shallow water thoughtfully chewing their cuds.) On one side of our cabin was old Mr. and Mrs. Dandison's cabin. They were the original occupants at Indian Lake, before any summer cabins were built. At first they lived in kind of a ramshackle green shingle-covered shack, but then later built a brand new, more modern cabin with a wide, enclosed front porch. (A few years later, we sold our log-sided cottage and bought this cabin from the Dandisons.) The Dandisons had numerous grandchildren who often came to visit from downstate in the summertime. There were Danny and Davy Dewey, who weren't twins, but almost, so alike were they. And there was a slim, brown-limbed girl named Cookie, who enchanted all of us boys, and often hung out with us on our porch, where we vied, probably none too subtly, for the place next to her, 'cause she was really cute, in a tomboy-ish kind of way.

On the other side of us was A.C. Rohe's cabin, a cinder block, half-basement affair built into the hillside. Rohes had four boys, Albert ("Junior" to most everyone then), Charles, Fred and Johnny.

The Dandison cottage next to ours on Indian Lake. We bought this place in 1957.

37

Mrs. Rohe, Barbara, was one of my mom's best friends from town, where their house was only a block away from ours. (Mom still remembers how, on the day we were moving into our Holdenville house from Potterville, Barbara came bearing fresh-baked cookies for us, still warm from the oven, to welcome us to the neighborhood.) Junior and Charles were close in age to my brothers Rich and Bill, and they spent a lot of time together at the lake, tinkering with an outboard-powered speedboat that the two elder Rohe boys had built themselves at home. They were constantly trying to come up with ways to tweak up the power on their motor to increase speed or improve its performance in boat races up and down the lake, or for pulling water skiers.

I spent a lot of time with Fred, although he was a few years younger than me, and we became fast friends. There was a play area up the hill near our cottages, with a set of swings and a slide, and a sandpit behind them, where we spent countless hours together, building roads and bridges and small villages in the sand and playing with our small toy cars and trucks.

The older boys sometimes poked fun at us for "playing in the sand," and often would come by and maliciously destroy our carefully constructed creations, kicking them to pieces with their bare or sneakered feet. They were just sand structures, after all. One day Rich had come through a couple of times already and kicked over our sand houses with his large bare feet. Upset by his meanness, Fred and I devised a plan to get even. Well, it was probably mostly my plan. We built another, much larger sand structure, and embellished it with carved windows and doors and turrets, and inside it we concealed a very large stone (actually, a small boulder we had rolled laboriously into place). It presented a most tempting target. When Rich came by the next time, I told him, "You better not smash *this* castle. It took a *lot* of work!" Unable to resist such a blatant challenge, Rich took a run at the target to get in a powerful kick this time. Well, fortunately he didn't break his foot, but he was hurting too much to chase us when Fred and I took off, laughing at his surprise and shock. He didn't mess with our stuff after that.

For the most part though, our summer days at Indian Lake were idyllic. Not many kids were as lucky as we were in that respect. As soon as school was out for the year, we packed up and moved to the lake for the summer. I suppose it might not have been such a wonderful deal for Mom, who still had cooking and cleaning and washing to do, but for us kids it was like heaven. Mom and Dad had taught us all to swim at an early age, so we had no fear of the water, and spent most of our days in it, cannonballing off the end of Rohe's dock, or diving off the raft out in the deeper water. Junior and Charles had made this raft out of castoff lumber and four sealed empty oil drums that acted as floats. It had a tall diving platform at one end and a ladder at the other. About the only time we weren't in the water swimming or playing was during that required "one hour after a meal," a concept that is no longer observed these days, I don't think. The prevailing belief at that time was that a full stomach could cause cramps and you could sink and drown. So we'd impatiently sit out that hour, asking Mom every five minutes or so, "Is the hour up yet?"

Apparently a bottle of pop wouldn't cause cramps, because one of our favorite pastimes while waiting out that hour was to sit under a tree and chug a bottle of Oh-So Good grape or orange soda, or an RC Cola (a preferred brand because of the bigger bottle), and then have belching contests, with points awarded for duration, volume, or "wetness" and richness of texture. My brother Bill was especially talented at this, and could quite distinctly burp words and even whole phrases like, "Hel-looo," and "How-do-you-doooo?" or "Eck-ska-yoooz-meee."

Tim and Bob at Indian Lake, circa 1954. Note Bob's athletic physique and Charles Atlas pose.

Altar Boys or
"The Church Story"

Yes, we were regular boys, and boys have always enjoyed any kind of humor involving burps, farts, and other bodily functions, or poop. We loved "scatological" humor long before we ever learned the word. And while we're on the subject, there's this horribly embarrassing thing that happened to me once, while engaged in a flatulence competition. It's not a story I'm anxious to tell, but if I don't include it in this – *my* story, after all – my brothers, Bob in particular, would be all over me like flies on fresh cow flop, wanting to know, "Why didn't you tell the church story?" "*Church story?!*" you might well ask. "What could burping, farting or poop possibly have to do with *church?*" Well, that's a reasonable question, so I'll try to give a reasonable explanation, but it will need a little background, so bear with me, please.

I haven't said anything about religion or church-going yet, but church was always a big part of our lives growing up. We're Catholic, and all of us attended St. Philip's Catholic School here in Reed City through the eighth grade. Back then, in the fifties and sixties, part of going to Catholic school was attending daily Mass every morning before classes.

Like all good Catholic boys of that era, my brothers and I were all trained as acolytes, or "altar boys," to assist the priest on the altar during Mass. This duty was considered an honor and a privilege, a matter that was duly impressed on all of us boys as we were "pressed" into service at around the age of eight or nine. Before that age, we probably couldn't have learned all the Latin prayers of response necessary to the all-Latin ritual that was observed at that time, before Vatican II and all the reforms and changes brought about by that council. As it was, we younger recruits often learned pidgin-Latin responses which the older boys taught us with completely straight faces, laughing surreptitiously up their surpliced sleeves as we innocently repeated back bogus responses like, "Me a cowboy, me a cowboy, me a *Mexican* cowboy" (instead of the Confiteor's proper, "Mea culpa, mea culpa, mea maxima culpa").

Does this mean that we didn't *believe* in the mumbo-jumbo that was the Latin Mass? No, we *did* believe – in our own unthinking boyish ways. It was just that Mass and being in church was such an ingrained part of our daily experience that we became casual about it. We were comfortable with it. It wasn't a case of familiarity breeding contempt, but simply the achievement of a certain comfort level in being in and out of the sacristies and the sanctuary practically every day. The brick and stone structure on Chestnut Street that was St. Philip's church was practically as familiar to us as altar boys as our own homes were.

Mass serving schedules were printed in the church bulletin every Sunday. Weekday masses only required two servers, and the

Interior of old St. Philip church, where we attended daily Mass before marching to school.

same two boys served for a week at a time. I was usually paired with my brother Bob, always an uneasy alliance at best. Weekday Masses began at 8:00. My dad would drop us off at the church around 7:30 on his way to work, so we would usually have more than enough time to make the necessary preparations for Mass: lighting the altar candles, filling the cruets with water and wine, laying out the priest's vestments – all this *after* the initial argument over who got to wear the best cassock and surplice (the acolyte's own "vestments") out of the oak wardrobe in the altar boys' sacristy.

At any rate, we often had nearly a half hour to kill in a nearly empty darkened church, so – I hate to say "boys will be boys," but they *will* be. And part of being boys, of course, is that aforementioned delight in vulgar humor and a healthy competitive spirit.

To wit, upon crossing the sanctuary together between the sacristies, as we genuflected before the altar, I inadvertently softly broke wind. Competitive spirit that he was, and has always been (a four-year letterman in college track years later), without missing a beat, Bob farted in response, but louder, and with a superior smirk. Rising to the challenge, I farted again, this time with a little extra oomph, so to speak, and easily topped Bob's effort. Bob responded with a really resounding feat of flatulence – the kind of fart that should have brought me to my knees in awe and obeisance, hailing him humbly as "Master!" But the gauntlet was down, the challenge had been made, and, inside the priest's sacristy by now, Bob was openly laughing in scorn at my puny toots, and already reveling in yet another victory over his clearly inferior younger brother.

I shouldn't have done it. I know that now, but I went for it. Tensing my abdominal muscles and grunting audibly, I bore down for the win, and – *"HOLY SHIT!"* (We *were* on hallowed ground, after all.) I *did* fart, and with admirable volume, but something was wrong. It felt way too *wet*, and I knew immediately that I'd gone too far. My sphincter had blinked, and my bowels had let loose. Like the old kid's joke (*more* scatological humor): Q: "Do you know what a surprise is?" A: "A fart with a lump in it." Well, I was surprised in spades. That hearty breakfast of hot cocoa and homemade buttered toast had done its work. Horrified, I exited the sacristy to the sound of Bob's "ee-YUUU" and incredulous

The old St. Philip Catholic church at corner of Chestnut and Bitner, June 1961.

laughter, frog-stepping spread-legged down the stairs into the church basement to the bathroom, where, door securely locked, I removed surplice, cassock and my trousers, and then, gingerly, my shit-streaked underpants, which I attempted to wash in the toilet. But then they were completely wet and unwearable. So, after cleaning myself off, I put back on my pants, which, fortunately were still clean. What I did with those soiled jockey shorts I have mercifully blotted from my memory bank, but, according to family legend (yes, the story has been oft repeated at family gatherings, particularly by Bob and Rich, who seemed to really enjoy the re-telling and often embellished on the truth), the underpants were recovered from a clogged toilet a day or two later by Fred Morris, the church janitor.

Not my finest moment, and one I will never live down, I'm sure. But now you know, as Paul Harvey would say, "the *rest* of the story."

And yes, I did serve Mass that morning, chastened, mortified and uncomfortably underpants-less, with Bob periodically sneaking looks at me, smirking and chortling quietly. You've probably heard the expression, "God'll get you for that." Well, He did. *My* irreverence was amply punished, but I always wondered, what about *Bob's* blasphemous irreverence? Oh, well, "judge not ..." (But God *will* get you one day, Bob.)

The preceding anecdote notwithstanding, we really *were* good Catholic boys, all of us. We were there for those Masses every morning, and then marched in formation the several blocks south down Chestnut to St. Philip's school for classes, until we graduated from the eighth grade. The school only stayed in operation for about twenty years. The diocese closed it down around 1970, but that was long enough for me and all my siblings to get a good grounding in Catholic education, for which we are eternally grateful.

Holdenville School:
Kindergarten and the Classics,
or "Adventures in Reading"

But St. Philip's wasn't my first school experience. No, my formal education began at the Holdenville School, which I only attended for one year. It was a one-room K-8 country school just a block north from our house. I was five years old and was in "beginners" grade, which was what they called it there, rather than kindergarten. But beginners was more than kindergarten. It wasn't just a socialization, or "everybody play nice, then take a nap" experience. No, we learned reading, our numbers and some basic math skills, in addition to the normal socialization skills.

It was 1949, and probably already the beginning of the end for many of these small country schools, which once flourished all over our country, particularly in sparsely populated, rural areas. By the end of the fifties, most of these relics of the frontier had closed their doors, and rural students were then bused to a central or consolidated school in the nearest town.

My teacher at Holdenville was Esther Stager, who was also our next-door neighbor to the south. Her husband John was a farmer and they had two children, Roger and Violet, also students in their mother's classroom and our sometime playmates. At the time I attended Holdenville School, there were probably around thirty-some students in all the grades combined. One might think that, with that many students, ranging in age from five to thirteen, all in one room, chaos would reign. Not so. Discipline was almost never a real problem, and lessons proceeded in an orderly fashion. Probably the main reason for this was that teachers were much-respected figures in the community then, much more so than is the case today, and if your parents heard that you'd caused any trouble at school or had been punished, then you'd get punished again when you got home. The only punishment I can recall being meted out in Mrs. Stager's classroom was being sent to sit in a corner, facing the wall – probably the equivalent of today's "time-out."

It was always orderly and "business-as-usual" during school hours. Each grade level got their share of the teacher's attention at given times, while the other children worked diligently on their assignments, or listened in on what was going on in the other grade-level recitations and activities, which was actually a good thing, as you often learned things beyond your own grade, absorbing knowledge and information at an unconscious level.

At any rate, I learned to read, and read well, by the time I completed beginners. The truth is, I can hardly remember ever *not* being able to read. I've had to consult with my higher authority on

Rich and Bill at Holdenville School, circa 1948.

such matters – Mom. I asked her if perhaps she might have taught me to read even before I started school. She doesn't remember any conscious effort to teach me to read, but did grant that, since she read to me, to all of us kids, on a regular basis when we were small, I may have picked up the rudiments of reading before school. For whatever reason,

1949 (age 5).

I mastered reading very quickly under Mrs. Stager's tutelage, and *loved* to read, and still do, passionately.

Reading was a key part of the "reward" system at Holdenville School. If a student finished his assignment early and had extra study time, he was allowed to go to a shelf at the back of the room and select something extra-curricular to read. There were a few children's books and biographies of famous people on this shelf, but by far the favorite books for extra reading were the comic books. But what *special* comic books these were! A firm called The Gilberton Company in New York published, in comic book form, a lengthy list of literary classics, which they aptly called *Classics Illustrated.* There were over 150 titles in print by the time the firm went out of business sometime in the late sixties. I know this because while I was in college it was my ambition to collect a complete set. Alas, I never did so, but still do own sixty or more of their titles. They probably wouldn't be very valuable from a collector's standpoint though, as they have been much read and enjoyed by me, my brothers and sister, and, later, by my own children.

Of course, reading a comic book edition of a literary masterpiece is no substitute for reading the complete original work, but these comics played a significant role in whetting my appetite for the real thing. By the time I advanced to first grade at St. Philip's, I already had a rudimentary knowledge of the plots and major characters of *The Three Musketeers, The Last of the Mohicans, Frankenstein, Oliver Twist, Uncle Tom's Cabin, Ivanhoe, The Adventures of*

1951 – Holdenville:
Tim, Bob, Mary, Bill and Mom

Huckleberry Finn, The Hunchback of Notre Dame, Twenty Thousand Leagues Under the Sea, and many other major works of world literature. Not your usual kindergarten reading list, to be sure.

So it was a little difficult to get excited about Dick and Jane and reading "See Spot run," after becoming personally acquainted with D'Artagnan and his stalwart fellow musketeers; or after traveling down the mighty Mississippi with Huck and Jim; or reading of the cruelty of the evil overseer, Simon Legree; or navigating the ocean depths aboard the Nautilus with the mysterious Captain Nemo. But I did read the Dick and Jane stories, along with the other kids, biding my time, knowing that after school I could read what *I* wanted to read. Because I continued to read voraciously in much of my spare time.

I discovered that *Classics Illustrated* comics were occasionally available in the local drugstores on the comic racks, and would beg Mom for money to buy one whenever I could. Of course, Mom loved literature too, and was no dummy. She recognized that these comics offered an attractive introduction to the real McCoy, so she was an easy mark.

I also learned, quite by accident, that the small general store in Oakley, where my Grandpa and Grandma Whalen still lived, regularly stocked *Classics Illustrated*, with quite a large selection of the titles. So during our visits there, whenever Grandma sent us to the store for milk or bread, we would also come away with a few new literary treasures, and would sprawl quietly on the floor for hours (Grandpa liked things quiet in the house), learning of Paris and Helen, Hector and Achilles, Odysseus and Penelope, the Trojan War and its aftermath. We made the acquaintance of young Jim Hawkins and Long John Silver; and read of Gulliver and the Lilliputians and Robinson Crusoe and his man Friday. We shivered in the frozen fastness of the far north with Buck and John Thornton, and learned the law of the club and fang. Oh, the places I could go, and the things I could do and see, all the while lying warm and secure in Grandma's parlour in the sleepy little hamlet of Oakley! And it all started with comic books.

By the time I was in the third and fourth grade, I was reading *real* books, the original versions of many of the same classics. After reading *The Call of the Wild, White Fang, Black Beauty,* and Marshall Saunders' *Beautiful Joe,* I became quite hooked on animal stories, particularly dog and horse stories. Luckily, there were plenty of such books for kids in print then. I read my way through all of Albert Payson Terhune's collie books, then Jack O'Brien's *Silver Chief* books and Eric Knight's *Lassie, Come Home.* I read Will James' *Smoky the Cowhorse,* Marguerite Henry's *King of the Wind* and *Misty of Chincoteague,* and all of Walter Farley's *Black Stallion* books. I read Ernest Thompson Seton's *Wild Animals I Have Known* and Felix Salten's original *Bambi,* and countless other such tales of adventure about animals and their special people.

One favorite author of this time, introduced to me by my mom and her folks was James Oliver Curwood, a native of Owosso and an early naturalist, who wrote numerous adventure tales set in the far north in the late nineteenth and early twentieth centuries. Some of his books aimed at children were *Kazan the Wolf Dog;* and *Baree, Son of Kazan.* Curwood Castle, the author's workplace in Owosso, was, and still is a popular tourist attraction. Unfortunately, most of his books are no longer in print.

Where did I get all these books to read, you might ask. Well, one of my favorite places in Reed City was the public library. It was then located on the southwest corner of Upton and Higbee, upstairs over the City Hall and the city police headquarters. I made weekly visits to the library throughout most of my childhood. It seemed to me a place of immense riches – all those books waiting to be read. I worked my way steadily through all the animal stories and many of the classics first introduced to me in comic book form, then sampled many of the series books, like *The Hardy Boys* and *Tom Swift,* although I never became addicted to those kinds of books.

In addition to the library books, our house was always filled with books and magazines too, as my mother was, and is, a reader, although when I was young she probably didn't have much spare time for reading. Nevertheless, she made sure that all her kids were exposed to books and reading opportunities from an early age. There were, at various times, subscriptions to *The Saturday Evening Post, Life, Reader's Digest, Catholic Digest, Woman's Day, Ladies' Home Journal, Boy's Life, Jack and Jill, Farm Journal, Popular Science,* and *Popular Mechanics,* in addition to daily and weekly newspapers, usually the *Grand Rapids Press, Osceola Herald,* and, sometimes, *Grit.* And we all looked forward to the periodic arrival of *Reader's Digest Condensed Books* too. My favorite presents for birthdays and Christmas were, of course, books, and my parents and grandparents kept me well supplied.

A couple *Saturday Evening Post* covers that I particularly remember were the Norman Rockwell portraits of presidential candidates Dwight D. Eisenhower and Adlai Stevenson, the former being the first president that really entered my consciousness, although I probably should remember something about Truman too. (And that's about as political as this memoir will get.)

Townview Farm:
Chickenshit, Pickles and Hay,
or "The Eggman Cometh"

Access to the downtown area and library became even easier for me in 1952, when we moved across town to West Church Avenue, on the southern edge of the city. Dad bought about twenty-five acres of land there, which included our "new" house, commonly referred to then as the "old Morefield place," and also a small farm ("the Pratt place"), with a house, barn, chicken coop and pigpen with shed.

Dad's plan, when he bought this acreage, with its little farm, was to move his mother and father up from Wayland, where they were then tenant farmers. This, I'm sure, was a matter he needed to handle very delicately, since he didn't want to wound his father's pride. So with Mom's help, Dad drafted a very diplomatic letter to his folks, explaining that he had this small farm now, but didn't have time to work it himself, and would really appreciate it if they would consider moving to Reed City, where Grandpa would be in charge of running the farm, and they would both have a place to live too, right near Mom and Dad and all us kids. Although my grandpa Bazzett had never enjoyed much success in his life, he was a very proud and stubborn man, and not inclined to accept anything that smelled like charity. Nevertheless, after some tactful

Our "new" house (aka "the old Morefield place) at 423 West Church, May 1952. Tim and Mary (one year-old) in foreground.

negotiations by Mom and Dad, and also, I'm sure, by Grandma, who was all for the move and overjoyed at the prospect of living so close to her grandkids, several months later, with some help from my uncles Don, Ken and Bernard, my grandparents moved into the farmhouse on West Church. They christened their new home "Townview Farm." It was 1953, a year also marked by the birth of my brother Chris, who was to be the last child in our family.

My grandparents' move was to have, I realized years later, a profound influence on my life, and it brought me closer to my dad's folks too. How did this change my life? First of all, I was about to become a "pseudo-farm kid." I feel I have to qualify my status with the "pseudo," because I was never subject to the grueling daily labor and responsibilities that I know were the lot of many of my school classmates, who lived on real subsistence farms throughout the country around Reed City and Paris. Instead, I kind of had the best of both worlds. I was a town kid, meaning I lived inside the city limits and could easily walk just about anywhere in town in fifteen or twenty minutes, like the library, the movie theater, the Dairy Queen, the ballfields, church or school. But on the other hand, I was now sort of a farm kid too, because, from the very beginning of my grandparents' taking up residency in Reed City, my brothers and I all assumed some responsibilities on "the farm."

Townview Farm on West Church. The house was razed in 1967, but barn still stands.

And make no mistake, it *was* a farm, with all the work, equipment, animals, crops, chores, dirt and odors usually associated with a farm. Grandpa brought along all the tools of his trade: a John Deere tractor, with its distinctive putt-putt chuff, a hay mower and rake, manure spreader, plow, drag, disc, seeder, corn planter, wagons, and numerous other implements and tools large and small. He also brought along livestock, most notably three Holstein cows: Merry, Beaulah and Judy. Yes, his cows had names. Grandpa would never have admitted it, but he had a soft spot for his cows.

Grandma and Grandpa Bazzett on back steps of their "Townview Farm" in Reed City, circa 1956.

Grandpa Bazzett's beloved bovines: Beaulah, Merry and Judy.

A stern, taciturn man, Grandpa kept to a rigid schedule, and, for the most part, never deviated from it as long as I knew him. He would rise every day around 5:00 and begin his round of chores: feeding the stock, milking the cows, mucking out the barn and other buildings, and, depending on the season, going out to work in the fields, or tending to maintenance and repairs of his tools and implements. He kept busy all day, every day, for as long as he lived. If he never attained much material or financial success during his lifetime, it wasn't due to a lack of hard work.

Grandpa was already white-haired and stooped by the time I came to know him. Years later I learned his stoop was the result of the constant pain and discomfort caused by a double hernia which he let go untreated for years. He had an old-fashioned ingrained distrust of doctors and hospitals, so instead of seeking treatment, he wore a mail-order truss for support, and became increasingly bent over as the hernias worsened.

Finally, after years of this suffering, he reluctantly gave in to my dad's constant urging to go into the hospital and undergo surgery to have the condition repaired. Grandpa was actually afraid of hospitals, and said, "People *die* in hospitals." Much to his surprise, however, he survived the operation. While he was still hospitalized, Dad and Rich moved Grandpa's bed from his upstairs bedroom downstairs into the unused dining room of the farmhouse, so he wouldn't have to climb the stairs for a few days when he came home. (This was another unexplained mystery to me as a kid. My folks slept in the same bed, but Grandpa slept upstairs and Grandma slept downstairs at their house.) Grandpa got home on a Saturday night and slept in the dining room, but on Sunday morning, while we were all at Mass with Grandma, he carried his bed back upstairs and put it "back where it belonged." So much for trying to make things easier for Grandpa.

But I've gotten way ahead of myself again. What were *my* jobs and responsibilities on the farm? I was nine when my grandparents arrived in Reed City. One of my primary daily jobs (shared with Bob) was to gather the eggs from the nests in the chicken coop We usually kept two or three dozen chickens at any given time. This wasn't my first experience with chickens either. We'd had a few chickens at our house in Holdenville too. I think, having grown up on a farm, Dad liked the "convenience" of producing our own eggs, which we all ate a lot of growing up. (We also kept a small number of turkeys one year in Holdenville, and I have a vivid memory of being chased across the yard by these tall fearsome-looking birds, and running up the back steps and and banging on the door, bawling for mama to "save me!" Turkeys are pretty brainless birds and will chase anything that runs, but *I* didn't know that.)

Anyway, I have to tell you about those damn chickens, and, in particular, that first rooster that Grandpa brought along with the original flock from Wayland. From day one that rooster had it in for me. He must have noticed a certain hesitance on my part when I entered the chicken house, because as soon as I'd gotten inside and closed the door behind me, he would burst raging and squawking from atop the roosts or behind the nesting boxes, running at me with neck extended and feathers fluffed, pecking and protesting. I would fend him off with my egg basket, and eventually he would back off and strut cockily away, eyeing me nastily over one shoulder. (Hmm ... do chickens *have* shoulders?) I quickly grew to dread these small confrontations, and, as a consequence, would open the door a small crack and peer in to try to locate the rooster before actually entering the coop.

One day Grandpa was coming across the barnyard and saw me peering into the barely cracked door, and came over and asked me what I was doing. Rather shamefacedly I explained what had been happening. Placing a hand gently on my shoulder, Grandpa said it was time to apply a little "animal psychology," then told me to go ahead on in and he'd be right behind me. A bit puzzled, but feeling better at Grandpa's presence, I opened the door and went in, Grandpa following. Right on cue, that rooster came raging out at me from underneath the roosts. Grandpa stepped swiftly around me, and, with a single perfectly measured step, he drop-kicked that damn rooster clear across the chicken house and up against the opposite wall in an explosion of feathers and noise. Subsiding shaken onto the floor, the rooster shook itself and wobbled shakily for shelter under the nests. Nodding his head in satisfaction, Grandpa solemnly informed me that that rooster wouldn't give me any more trouble. And he was right. This was my first (and only) lesson in animal psychology according to Juda, but a lesson that I remembered – at least when it came to chickens.

Rich with Wayne, a calf first raised in a pen in Kent Elevator office, then brought to Townview Farm as a beef steer - circa 1960.

There was never any love lost between me and chickens. Once they've outgrown that fuzzy yellow chick stage, there's absolutely nothing cute or cuddly about chickens. They are filthy, foul, beady-eyed creatures whose only saving grace is that they produce eggs, one of nature's most perfect (and tasty) foods. You know that old riddle: "Which came first, the chicken or the egg?" Well, as far as I was concerned when I was the West Church chickenmaster, I heartily wished it were the egg, because I sure could have done without all those damn chickens.

In addition to gathering the eggs, Bob and I were tasked with keeping the chickens fed and watered and with periodically mucking out the coop, a really filthy job we usually tried to put off, but couldn't, because chickens are undoubtedly the shitting-est creatures on the face of the earth. And chicken shit is one of the foulest ("fowl-est?") forms of shit too. It crusts and dries and flakes and forms a powder that floats in the air and can get in your lungs. We had to scrape the roosts and any other horizontal surfaces clean of the stuff, then put down lime. We forked up all the shit-splattered straw from the floor and nests and wheelbarrowed it out into the barnyard to the manure pile, then spread fresh straw on the floor and put clean straw into the nest boxes. It was truly nasty work. We wore kerchiefs over our noses and mouths to try to keep the shit and dust and chaff out of our lungs. Yeah, it was a shitty job, "but somebody had to do it," as the saying goes.

The upside of the job (if there *was* an upside) was the egg business. The chickens supplied many more eggs than our family needed, so the surplus eggs had to be cleaned, candled, sized and cartoned for distribution and sale. Bob and I got to split the proceeds of these sales. Since eggs sold for thirty or forty cents a dozen at the time, it probably wasn't all that much, but it was something to show for all our efforts. We had several regular customers right in the neighborhood. We delivered eggs right to the door for the Petersons, Hendersons, Gordons, Mays, Ignatoskis and others.

We also had the cows and a few pigs on the farm, but I can't remember having any regular responsibilities for those. Grandpa took care of the cows himself for the most part, although I know

Grandpa B. and his pigs circa 1954. Grandma wrote on back of photo: "Raising hogs again! ... Come up and eat some pork chops with us!"

Rich and Bill helped sometimes too, and learned to milk the cows, in case Grandpa couldn't. I never really did any of the milking, except for one time, when I tried it, at Dad's urging, when he was helping out in the barn one day. He showed me how to place the bucket under the cow's udder, then pull the short, three-legged milking stool right up to the cow's side and hunker down on it and even lean your head up into the cow's warm flank, murmuring soothingly while firmly grasping a teat in each hand. Well, I never got much beyond that point in the instructions, because just as I got myself tenuously situated, the cow took a step back and down into the gutter that runs behind the stalls. The cow's udder dropped as she stepped down, and, panicking, thinking I'd pulled too hard, I exclaimed, "Dad! The cow's bag fell off into the bucket!" Chuckling, Dad took over, and that was pretty much the end of my short-lived milking career, but Dad never tired of telling that story to anyone who would listen, particularly to his farmer customers at the elevator, much to my everlasting embarrassment and chagrin.

I also never had much to do with the pigs, but we usually had three or four pigs around, which were fed all manner of garbage, along with measured rations of Wayne Feeds "Tail Curler," that Dad brought home from the elevator. Grandpa kept a garbage pail inside his back porch, where the milk separator was also kept. He would pour the skimmings from the milk over the potato peelings, coffee grounds and other garbage and table scraps in this bucket. Then I, or whoever was around at the time, would tote the brimming bucket of "slops" down the hill to the pigpen and pour it into the trough, much to the pigs' noisy, grunting delight. Since eventually these pigs got eaten themselves, feeding them these slops was an early form of recycling – "waste not, want not."

I remember a litter of piglets that our sow dropped one year. Now piglets really are cute when they're new, but they don't stay small or cute for long. One day when they were still small-to-medium size, Dad sent Milt Steinhaus, one of his hands at the mill, up to the farm to do a bit of unpleasant "hog maintenance." Milt brought along his trusty jackknife, which he was forever sharpening in his spare moments. It was time to ring the pigs' noses and castrate the young boars. It was a messy business all around, but was one of Milt's special skills. I remember him coming to our pigpen in Holdenville too, when I was quite small, to help slaughter a hog there. It's necessary to put rings in pigs' noses as a deterrent to keep them from rooting their way under the fences or doing other damage, since a pig's snout can be a powerful and destructive digging implement. The insertion of a metal ring into the septum of the pig's snout makes this destructive behavior a most uncomfortable experience, so rooting is all but eliminated.

Milt's method of castrating was a simple and straight forward one. He would slit open the shoat's scrotum, pop out and slice free the testicles, then apply a tarry-looking ointment to seal the wound and prevent infection. All of this was executed in a rapid and efficient one-two-three fashion perfected by years of experience. Milt was also called upon by many local farmers to castrate young bulls or to geld colts. I hesitate to say he actually enjoyed this work, but I think he did. It was, after all, a necessary and hard-won skill, and he took a justifiable pride in doing it well. A few years later, when I began working part-time at the mill, Milt would teach me many useful things.

Cows, pigs, chickens – these were part of my education on the farm. I learned to think of them all as part of the food chain. This was easy enough with the pigs and the chickens, but you could get attached to the cows, with their deep brown eyes and their obvious pleasure at being rubbed on their broad foreheads between those eyes. And you ain't never been kissed, 'til you been kissed by a cow. In addition to our usual two or three milk cows, we also raised a steer for beef a couple of summers, just turning it loose in the pasture to graze, with a regular grain ration to help fatten it, then we would slaughter it in the fall.

A cow kept for one summer specifically designated for beef was one thing, but it was quite another thing some years later, when Grandpa's beloved milkers, Merry, and then Beaulah, reached the end of their productive years and were also slaughtered for beef. The meat was processed and packaged at the local locker plant. Dad would mark the white, butcher paper packages with the cut of meat and the cow's name, then store it in our huge chest freezer in the basement. My brothers and I would all slightly wince when, at supper, Dad would ask Mom, concerning a roast or hamburgers we were eating, "Is this Merry or Beaulah? It's really *good*!" But such is life (and death) on a family farm.

Haying time on West Church, circa 1957. Grandpa Bazzett driving his John Deere, Rich up on top, Tim and Bob on tailgate, Mary running behind.

The livestock was only a part of the farm package though. Dad – and Grandpa too – were determined to make this as productive and self-supporting an operation as possible. And in retrospect I often wonder if Dad also wanted to be sure that his own kids got a thorough taste of what it's like to work the land and grow things and use their hands. If that was his intention, it certainly worked. If we had not had those experiences, we would have been exceedingly different people, I think. I am personally convinced that we are better people because of our "farm experience."

But I digress. There was a wide variety of tasks to be done on Grandpa's farm. There was the plowing, dragging, discing and fertilizing that prepared the land for various crops. These were tractor-driven tasks that Grandpa usually handled himself, although Rich assumed some of those jobs as he got older. And then there was the planting – of field corn, oats, alfalfa, rye, timothy and other varieties and blends of hay and forage crops, all to feed the stock.

Haying was usually accomplished in the worst heat of summer, and was dusty, gritty, grueling work. Like most crops, once hay is ripe and ready to be cut, you often have a rather small window of time to get it out of the field and into the barn, if you want optimum quality hay. It's a multi-stage operation that can take several days or more, depending on the acreage involved, and you hope like hell the weather cooperates. Sunshine and breezes are helpful, because once the hay is cut, it needs to be raked into windrows so it can dry out before it is baled or loaded loose onto a wagon and transported to a barn for storage. (Keep in mind that the methods I'm describing here are those of forty or more years ago. Today there are more modern methods that streamline the process immensely.) If the hay is wet or too green when it is harvested, it can ferment after it's stored in the barn, causing intense heat to build up, particularly in tightly baled hay, resulting in a fire, called "spontaneous combustion." Once this happens, the whole stored hay crop can quickly go up in flames, often destroying the barn and everything in it, something every farmer feared.

We didn't have a lot of acreage in hay, since we only kept a few cows, but we still faced that same small window of opportunity to get our hay in, so it would be accurate to say we worked our asses off during haying time, and hoped for the best. The first few years we put up hay there was no baler involved, probably because Dad didn't want the expense of hiring one. We hand-loaded the hay. Once it had been cut and raked and had dried for a day or two, Grandpa, my brothers and I would move down the windrows with pitchforks, separating the rows into small piles of hay, a practice called "cocking the hay" (a small haystack is called a "haycock"). Then, when that was done, we would begin "getting in" the hay. Usually Bill would drive the tractor pulling the hay rack or wagon slowly down the field. Grandpa would be up on the wagon to "build the load." Rich, Bob and I (and whomever else we could round up to help) would fork the hay up onto the wagon, where Grandpa would spread it into evenly overlapping layers so it wouldn't slide back off the rack, no mean feat in itself. Initially, the going was rather easy, but after several turns up and down the field, the load grew higher and higher, until you were forking the hay high over your head to get it up onto the load to Grandpa. Once the top of the load was out of reach, it was time to head for the barn.

Our hayfields were mainly situated in a small valley south of the house and barn, so there was a gradual incline we had to negotiate with our tractor and laden hayrack. We had two tractors on the farm, Grandpa's standard-sized John Deere and a smaller Farmall "Cub," which we sometimes used to pull the haywagon.

Grandpa Bazzett again with his John Deere, along with Bill, Chris and Mary

But you had to be careful not to overload the wagon when the lighter weight Cub was pulling it. I remember one particular occasion when we must have just slightly overtaxed the little tractor, because, as we chugged slowly up the grade, the engine began to shake and vibrate, and then suddenly the front wheels lifted off the ground and the tractor's nose began to rear into the air as the rear wheels continued to churn. Rich was driving the Cub, and his face went white as he realized the tractor was in real danger of upending itself. Luckily, Milt Steinhaus was working with us that day and was walking up the hill alongside the tractor. Acting quickly, he threw down his fork and leapt up onto the the tractor's nose, adding just enough weight to counterbalance the load and bring the front wheels back to earth. Laughing and hollering, "Ride, 'im, Rich!" he hung on like a bulldogger bringing down a steer, until the tractor reached leveler ground and stabilized. What may seem comical now, in retrospect, was actually an accident averted, and one that could easily have proven fatal, for farmers are often killed this way, when a tractor turns turtle on top of them. Although a bit shaken, Rich stayed in the saddle and brought the load in safely.

Unloading the hay from the wagon into the barn loft, or haymow, was another dusty, sweaty and suffocating job. It was actually worse than loading the hay, because it was an operation that was done entirely in an enclosed space, inevitably unbearably hot, up under the barn roof, with the dust and chaff swirling all around you, getting down your neck and under your clothes, into your eyes, nose and mouth and down your throat into your lungs. The dust was probably worse when you were mowing away loose hay, but, conversely, when we began baling our hay, the bales were often so heavy that it took a harsher toll on all your muscles, first heaving the bales up onto the wagon in the field, then up into the haymow for stacking. Either way, a day of haying always left you unutterably filthy and absolutely exhausted.

There were a couple of years when I was in my teens that the Bazzetts joined forces with the Eichenbergs, another large-ish family from our parish who also had a small family farm. Three of them and four of us made for more hands and quicker work of the haying, so after our hay was in, we'd travel over to their place on South Roth and repeat the process, until their hay too was safely mowed away in their barn. Often it would be fully dark by the time we finished, but, anxious to shed all the chaff, dirt and dust, we'd all pile into a car or two and drive the twelve miles out to Indian Lake and jump into the water to get clean and blessedly cool again. It was a wonderful and refreshing way to end a day of back-breaking labor.

The Eichenbergs and Bazzetts were always pretty close friends. George worked at Remenap's Hardware, right next to the Kent Elevator, in addition to working his farm. He and Violet raised their own help for the farm work, and their kids were born in near tandem with ours. Mary Lou Eichenberg was about Rich's age, Tom was in Bill's grade, Paul was Bob's age, and Keith and I were classmates, and close friends from first grade at St. Philip's onward. Later, their Larry was my sister Mary's age and Steve was Chris's age. Then Eichenbergs had two more kids than we did – Mark and Charlotte. Eichenbergs 8, Bazzetts 6 – they won. By today's standards, our families would be seen as unconscionably large, but back then we were just looked upon as "good Catholic families."

In addition to the hay and field crops, we also grew one "money crop" for a few years – cucumbers, or pickles, as we usually called them, probably because "pickle patch" has a more alliterative and pleasing sound than cucumber field. Admittedly, it wasn't much of a cash crop, but was one more tedious undertaking to keep us boys busy and out of trouble. (Although I can't imagine any kind of serious trouble we could have gotten into in Reed City.) Cucumbers took a lot of work. After the planting, you had to keep them watered and weeded and hoed until they blossomed and the blossoms became fruit ... er, vegetables. Then finally, there was the picking. *God*, I hated picking pickles! The only efficient way to do the job was to straddle the row of vines all bent over (in order to see the cukes hiding under the leaves), and, dragging your bucket beside you, work your way down the row as quickly as possible. When your bucket was full, you'd empty it into a burlap bag, then go back and do it again, over and over, until your back felt broken and your throat was parched from thirst from the hot sun beating down on you. Occasionally, to alleviate the tedium, we'd chuck soft overripe cukes at each other, but usually we were too tired for even that.

Bob was probably the best picker of all of us boys. He kept strict track of his share of the pickings and was probably always calculating how much money he stood to make from this picking and how many more pickings the vines might yield before the end of the season and how much he would be able to add to his bank balance by summer's end, with his pickle proceeds, egg money and whatever he might earn by peddling sweet corn and other fresh garden vegetables door-to-door in town, another money-making enterprise we shared when we had surplus produce. At any rate, Bob was one helluva pickle picker.

Once the pickles were picked and bagged, we took them to the "pickle plant" to sell. It wasn't really a "plant" or factory per se. It was a big barn at Glen Keller's farm just north of town. Inside, you'd weigh your pickles and then they were dumped out onto a big platform and pushed onto a system of moving belts and sorters that separated the cukes by size, so they could then be taken to a real plant to be further processed into dill or sweet pickles. The money we'd get was never that important to me. I was just glad to see the last of those damn pickles – until the next picking.

But they kept growing, as did the hay, the corn, the beans and all the crops that we planted and cultivated on the farm, and the seasons changed and the cycle continued. And so did I grow, as I absorbed the lessons of the land and of life that the farm taught me. I learned, however reluctantly, responsibility, probably the most important thing my dad tried so hard to inculcate into all of us. His constant mantra, repeated throughout all the years we were growing up, was: "First you do your *work*. *Then* you can play or rest." How I grew to hate that refrain. But it sank in, and became an integral part of who I am. Years later, I found myself repeating the same words to my own kids, particularly when they didn't do the few chores they were assigned to do. Even today, in retirement, I find myself unable to sit and relax with a book or the TV until *after* I've done some chores around the house, even if it's only washing up the dishes, running the vacuum or cutting the grass. Dad's lessons stuck, and, for me, there is no rest like an earned rest.

Beans and Bread
on Fridays

But my childhood wasn't just work and discipline. There were good times and certain family traditions that loom large in my memory of those times too.

For most of the years I was growing up on West Church Avenue, Fridays were a big deal at our house, not just because they marked the end of the school or work week, but because we were Catholic, and in those days before Vatican II Catholics were still forbidden to eat meat on Fridays. I suppose there was some good Church reason for this, like "mortification of the flesh," or to impose some small weekly penance or something. But for the Bazzetts, it didn't work. We didn't feel any hardship. Quite the opposite, we *loved* Fridays. Here's why: it was bread-baking day at our house. Mom would spend much of the day mixing and kneading and punching down the dough, giving it time to rise and all those other mysterious (to me) stages and machinations needed for the creation of home-baked bread. And, all the time while she was preparing and baking the bread, there was also a large pot of beans simmering on the back burner of the range, because Friday was "beans on bread" for supper, a Bazzett tradition.

On Thursday night Mom would get out a few pounds of navy beans, sort through them for any pebbles, then leave them in the big pot filled with water to soak overnight. Then the next day, adding salt and butter judiciously, she'd set the beans on the stove to boil and simmer all day while she baked bread.

Ah, that *bread*! *Mom's* bread! – the absolutely heavenly smells that wafted through our house on Fridays. My brothers and I would get off the St. Philip's school bus at its first stop at the corner of Chestnut and Church in front of Gondike's Gulf station, and literally *race* each other those two blocks home up Church, because Mom would set aside one medium loaf of hot-out-of-the-oven bread for an after-school treat for us. Whoever came crashing through the door first got first dibs on the heel of the loaf, or the crust, as we called it. Since I was usually dead last, being the youngest, I didn't really develop a taste for the end of a loaf until later in life. Mom would slice that whole loaf into thick steaming slices, slather on the butter (none of that new-fangled oleo-margarine on *our* bread), which quickly melted into the hot bread, and set out a plate with two pieces each for all four of us. Oh, the *ecstasy* of that hot buttered bread! Nothing compared to it. It was the perfect end of a week of school and work.

But that bread and beans kept right on working all week. Let me explain. Friday night our meatless supper usually consisted of beans on bread as the main dish. This is no doubt an acquired taste, or a dish you have to grow up eating. First of all, beans were cheap. Being in the elevator business, Dad got them wholesale, and we consumed vast quantities of beans in various forms and incarnations at our house. At any rate, boiled navy beans, served in their own buttery salted juices over buttered homemade bread, was considered a real delicacy at *Chez* Bazzett. Each of us boys could usually consume three or four servings of beans on bread, which was usually served with a Waldorf salad on the side.

Of course, all those beans, once eaten, expanded inside your stomach and digestive tract, leaving you feeling stuffed and bloated. Noxious natural gases would form that had to get out, and they did. Another advantage of beans then was their entertainment value, as we boys would try to outdo each other in raunchy, sometimes putrid-smelling farting contests a few hours after supper. Dad used to joke that we could have heated the house with all the gas generated by those beans.

But there's more. Since Mom cooked such a large quantity of beans all at once, there were usually plenty left over after Friday suppers. These beans were saved and re-used in a baked bean casserole (with sugar, bacon and molasses added) for Sunday dinner. We all loved Mom's baked beans too, so – more entertainment on Sundays. The remains of Sunday's baked beans were also carefully saved and refrigerated, and would show up later that week in our lunches as baked bean sandwiches, also a popular palate-pleaser in our family. Yeah, the Bazzetts loved their beans, and we all learned early in life the truth and the fun of the old axiom, "Beans, beans, the musical fruit. The more you eat, the more you toot."

Family portrait, Thanksgiving 1955.
L-R: Dad, Tim, Bill, Rich, Bob, Mom. Chris and Mary on laps. Our family was complete.

Grandpa Whalen:
Our Oldest Playmate

Another reason we had for liking Fridays was that it was usually the day when, at least four or five times a year, Grandma and Grandpa Whalen would show up for a weekend visit. Now while Grandma Whalen was okay, and would listen to us and marvel at our school accomplishments and praise us, Grandpa Whalen was like a really special treat for all of us. He was more like an overgrown mischievious playmate than a grownup. He wasn't at all like Grandpa Bazzett, who lived just across the field and whom we saw every day, and was always busy with his chores around the farm. Grandpa Whalen was retired. When he came to visit, he had nothing better to do than play with us kids, and we loved him for this. He would play cards with us for hours, mostly five-hundred rummy, of which he taught us all the rudiments, then he would blithely disregard many of the rules he had just taught us, and cheat with a perfectly straight face, so of course he almost always won. Mom thought it was just awful the way he cheated and took advantage of his own grandkids, but we didn't care, because he was giving us something so precious to us – his time and attention.

When we'd get home from school and find Grandpa and Grandma Whalen there for a visit, it would almost eclipse the pleasure of the usual fresh bread Friday treat. The first thing we'd always ask them was, "When are you going home?" which Mom said was an exceedingly rude thing to ask a guest. Of course, what we really *meant*was, *How long can you stay?* As soon as we'd gobbled down our bread and butter, we'd be after Grandpa to get out the cards and games, and he'd usually be glad to oblige. Sometimes we'd play Parcheesi or dominoes or Anagrams. Grandpa was equally adept at cheating and altering the rules to suit himself in almost any game. Although this "skill" sometimes left us a little confused, we'd soldier on, having fun, as long as Grandpa kept on playing with us.

Grandpa and Grandma Whalen visit in Holdenville, circa 1950.

Grandpa was plagued with asthma for as long as we knew him, so he had a special kind of wheezing laugh that we grew to know and love, and learned to emulate. He would chuckle at his small, contrived victories in our card games, and, tallying up the scores after each hand, would often say things like, "Hmm, looks like Tim's suckin' hind tit. Hee-hee-hee!" – much to our shocked delight. (Hee, hee, hee! Grandpa said, *tit!*)

Grandpa also liked to "go for rides." He bought a new car every few years and took an obvious pride in keeping it clean and polished, and enjoyed prowling the country roads around town, taking us boys along with him. A favorite route was out along the Cedar Road, east of town, that had a number of steep, rolling hills. At the top of a hill Grandpa would switch off his engine and put in the clutch and roll down the hill and partway up the next one, then pop the clutch and re-start the engine and continue on. This seemed like a kind of mechanical wizardry to us non-drivers, and our obvious wonder tickled Grandpa to no end.

He also liked to stop along the way on these country rides and "explore" old abandoned houses and shacks. One place we examined was a landmark of sorts for our family on our drive out to Indian Lake. It was a tiny, weathered shack located off in a

Grandpa Whalen and Mary-Jane, circa 1954.

grassy swale west of the Cedar Road. We always called it Apple Mary's place, as Dad had told us an old woman had once lived there all alone, surrounded by a small grove of stunted apple trees. It was just a one-room shack with a crude cellar dug underneath it and a tiny outhouse off to one side. There wasn't really much to "explore." Another place we explored was the old abandoned Tetzlaff house down a two-lane track in a small valley of sand and scrub growth. The drive was clearly marked NO TRESPASSING, but Grandpa said that didn't mean us, so we boys piled out of the car at the bottom of the trail and went inside the crumbling old house and poked around looking for several minutes. When we emerged from the house, Grandpa was *gone!* Panicking at the thought of being "lost in the wilderness," my brothers and I started running up the trail, calling, "Grandpa, where *are* you? Come *back*!" Just a few yards back up the trail, we spotted the car parked behind some bushes, Grandpa still sitting behind the wheel, wheezing and hee-hee-ing to beat the band. "Did you think I left you?" he chortled. Just another example of Grandpa's teasing sense of humor, but after that we were a little more cautious about letting him out of our sight on these explorations.

Another new treat that Grandpa Whalen introduced us to, when we went to visit him and Grandma in Oakley, was drive-in movies. Grandpa loved his car and he loved movies too, so drive-ins were a natural fit for him – and for us kids too. There was a drive-in theater in Owosso, less than a half hour south of Oakley, and we went there with Grandpa several times. He took us to see films *he* liked, not particularly caring if they were suitable for children. I remember seeing Anita Ekberg, the Swedish blonde bombshell, in *Back from Eternity*, in Grandpa's company. Va-va-

voom, hot stuff! Lotsa luscious deep cleavage in that one. We also saw the musical western, *Calamity Jane*, starring Doris Day and Howard Keel. I went around for days afterward, trying to duplicate Keel's masterful baritone, singing, in my prepubescent squeak, "My heart is *HIGH-er* than a hawk," or "I can do *ANY-thing* better than you can." I fell instantly in love with Doris Day, and I still love all the music from that film, which featured such other great songs as "Secret Love" and "The Deadwood Stage."

Yeah, Grandpa Whalen was always a treat for us when we were small. I think my mom may have resented it just a teensy bit that we loved him so much and followed him around like puppies. When she was a kid she remembers him being rather mean, stingy and self-centered. This may have been true, but Grandpa was one of those men who, while perhaps a lousy father, later mellowed into the ideal grandfather, and we loved him unreservedly for all the time he spent with us.

Uncles, Aunts and Cousins

Our extended family was never a particularly close one, partly because my uncles and aunts and cousins lived in different and rather distant cities, but mostly because my dad and mom just weren't all that close to their siblings. My mom's two brothers and their passel of kids – my Whalen cousins – we just never saw too much of. They lived in Owosso and Saginaw. My dad's brothers and the Bazzett cousins we didn't see much more of, although I can remember a few isolated visits.

One summer, when I was nine or ten, my Uncle Don and Aunt Isabel and their kids came and spent a weekend with us at our Indian Lake cabin. Their kids had a great time swimming and playing with us, so Don offered to take Bob and me back to their place in Lansing for the week, to spend some more time with our cousins, Donna, Ron and Duane. Mom and Dad decided that would be okay, and Bob and I were all for it, so we packed into Uncle Don's car on Sunday night and went home with them for a week's vacation in the big city.

A few things stand out in my memory from that one extended visit to Uncle Don and Aunt Isabel's place. Their house wasn't a real big one. Bob and I slept upstairs in Ron and Duane's room on pallets made up on the floor, since there were only two twin beds. This, of course, was no hardship, at that age. Quite the opposite; it was like a camping-out adventure.

Uncle Don & Aunt Isabel with Ronny & Donna Jean Circa 1945.

At the top of the stairs in their house, under the sloping ceiling, Uncle Don had his ham radio station and log books listing his far-flung radio contacts around the world. He let us listen in on a few broadcasts, and showed us how he tapped out Morse code callsigns and callups, and explained about getting licenses to broadcast in both Morse and voice, all pretty fascinating and exotic to us country boys. Another of Don's passions was hunting and fishing, and I remember sitting with the whole family one night that week to watch Mort Neff's *Michigan Outdoors*, a very popular TV show in the nineteen-fifties, which presented various features on hunting, fishing and camping weekly.

What I remember most about Aunt Isabel that visit, in addition to her sunny disposition and sweet smile, are her cucumber sandwiches, a delicacy I'd never tasted before then (despite all those damn pickles I'd picked). They were nothing more than sliced fresh cukes with salt and mayo on buttered white sandwich bread, but they seemed at the time like the perfect refreshing summer lunch. And I still associate cucumber sandwiches with fine summer days and Aunt Isabel.

And those really were halcyon summer days and nights for us. During the day we walked with Ron and Duane to the local municipal swimming pool to swim. Although Bob and I had been swimming since we were five or six years old, this was our first time ever in a large public pool. All our swimming had been done

A dapper-looking Uncle Ken, probably circa 1937

in lakes, where there weren't many rules to worry about. Older cousin Ron clued us in that the main thing to remember was , "Don't pee in the pool." That was easy enough to remember. But the first time I went down the water slide, I went so fast that I was all of a sudden under water, in all that chlorine, and I almost *did* piss myself, it was such an unfamiliar shock. But we quickly adjusted and had a great time swimming and splashing and diving in "our first pool" experience.

Other afternoons we would go downtown to the movies. All the people and traffic of Lansing was a bit intimidating to us Reed City boys, but the magic of movies made it worthwhile. One film we saw was Dean Martin and Jerry Lewis, in *Jumping Jacks*, wherein Dean and Jerry joined the paratroopers – more fodder for our fertile imaginations and future games.

While we were in Lansing, we also visited my Uncle Ken's workplace, a gasoline and service station, where we surreptitiously rode up and down on the car hoists and sniffed the marvelous, enveloping aroma of gas fumes. All things considered, our one trip to visit our Lansing cousins was a memorable one and a great success, but for some reason we never did it again.

Two of my dad's brothers – Ken and Vern – were combat veterans of World War II, elevating them to a lofty status in the eyes of their Reed City nephews. Our other uncle, Bernard, was too young for the war, being twenty years younger than my dad (but he did three years in the Army, all at Camp McCoy, Wisconsin, after the war). Dad hadn't served either, since he was already past thirty, but mostly because he was considered the sole support of his own growing family and also his parents at the time the United States entered the war. I think Uncle Don was similarly exempted from military service. But Ken had served in the Navy, and Uncle LaVerne, or just Vern, as he was called, was a tail-gunner in the Army Air Corps.

Uncle Vern, the tail-gunner, was the one who most captured our imaginations when we were kids, because, not only was he a war veteran, with several medals to his credit, he was also an *ex-con*! Yeah, Uncle Vern was kind of the black sheep of the family, and the source of much heartache to his folks. He was a drinker and a hothead, a bad combination, and he was evidently a pretty mean drunk, and got into some nasty brawls

Grandma Bazzett and Army Air Corps Tail-Gunner, Uncle Vern, circa 1945.

that finally landed him in prison. By the time we got to know him a little, he had been paroled. He was also divorced, something that lowered his status even more in our Catholic family.

However, in spite of all these strikes against him, Vern was still quite the charmer and something of a self-styled ladies' man, with his wavy red hair, freckles and quick smile. I remember one visit he made to our house on Church Street when I was about twelve. He came to visit his folks, Grandma and Grandpa Bazzett, and arrived with flowers for Grandma, and some for Mom too. He was driving a "new used" car he was quite proud of, and wearing a suit and tie, so he cut quite a dashing figure. After he'd been there a while, after Sunday dinner, he offered to take Bob and me to the movies, which Mom and Dad agreed to, somewhat reluctantly, I suspect, as they probably weren't sure yet whether Vern could be trusted.

The Reed Theater in town wasn't good enough for Vern; he took us all the way to Big Rapids, wanting to show off his car and get it up to "highway speed," which was fine with Bob and me. I don't think Vern cared what was showing at the movies, but, as it happened, the featured movie that Sunday was *Tea and Sympathy*, a wonderful film that dealt sensitively with the themes of adultery and homosexuality. Although I'm sure I didn't entirely understand all the implications of the film, I thought it was a great story, and fell half in love with Deborah Kerr. From my perspective, our outing with Uncle Vern was a complete success. However, when we returned home, Mom asked us what movie we saw, and when we told her, she immediately checked the title on the Catholic Legion of Decency movie listing, and was horrified to learn that her boys had just viewed a C-rated, or *condemned* movie! Another strike against poor Uncle Vern, who probably wasn't even aware of any such classifications for films. At any rate, Bob and I had thoroughly enjoyed the movie and our afternoon with Vern and continued to think he was an okay guy. (And I was always pretty skeptical about the moral judgment of the Legion of Decency after that too.)

Aunt Mary and Ucle Bernard's wedding photo 1956.

It was around this same time that my dad's youngest brother, Uncle Bernard, got married, down near Grand Rapids. Bob and I were altar boys at the nuptial mass, and our whole family was, of course, invited to the wedding and reception. Bernard married Mary Pawlowski, a beautiful girl from a large Polish-American family, and it was my first experience with a Polish wedding, a truly gala affair, with lots of drinking and dancing of polkas. It was a memorable occasion, and I have to admit I was much smitten with my new Aunt Mary, with her dark hair and eyes, dazzling smile and an almost regal kind of serenity. Indeed, eight children and nearly fifty years later, Aunt Mary remains one of the loveliest ladies I have ever known.

St. Philip School 1950-1958:
Stuff and "Nun-Sense"

Okay, I think I've dwelt long enough on family, summertime, and games we played. I should probably get back to how I got educated in the midst of all this fun. It wasn't just Dad and Mom who instilled values and put the "fear of the Lord" into me. There were also the School Sisters of Notre Dame, the teaching order of nuns who staffed St. Philip's School. They were the law at St. Philip's, and loomed large in the developing psyches of every child who ever entered those doors, whether they stayed just a few years, or for the full eight years of grammar school.

I can still remember my excitement about starting school at St. Philip's. Part of that initial excitement was due to the fact that I would ride a *bus* to school , a red, white and blue school bus that stopped right at the end of our driveway. Rich, Bill and Bob had already been riding that bus, but now it was *my* turn. It was 1950 and I was six years old and entering first grade. This year I would board that bus with my brothers and wave good-bye to Mom, standing in the driveway in her housedress and apron, suddenly alone in the house for the first time in years. (Now *that* is something I had never thought about until this very moment. That must have been quite an adjustment for Mom, perhaps even a rather wrenching one, seeing her "baby" off to school on the bus.)

St. Philip School, probably circa 1960.

Our bus driver was Barney Kailing, a Catholic farmer with red hair and beard who drove the bus to make a little cash. Of course, we called him "Mister" Kailing (adults– *any* adult – commanded respect in those times), but I'd never known anyone named "Barney" before, and it always confused me just a little, since Barney got on the bus and made his rounds fresh (or "redolent") from the barn and doing his morning chores. He always smelled faintly of cows, manure and other barn smells, hence my confusion over his rather exotic (to me, at least) name. Barney was a tobacco chewer too, and he kept a Maxwell House coffee can near his driver's seat to spit into when necessary, another strange and mysterious habit to me and some of the other first-timers on the bus. Barney was a shy and gentle soul though, and a stutterer. Whenever Mom or any other mothers or the nuns had anything to say to him, he would duck his head, blush and stammer, and "yes-um" or "no-um" in reply. He also had a kind and thoughtful side. One year when all my brothers and me were sick with the mumps, then my dad got them too, Barney came by to see how Dad was doing. He explained he wasn't afraid of catching anything, saying, "I've already had the mu-mu-mu-, the mumps."

My teacher for first and second grades was Sister Mary Osmond. Today, many nuns retain their own names after taking vows, but in the fifties, at least in the SSND order, each nun took the name of a saint, preceded, of course, by the name of Our Lady,

Mary. Manners and respect, which our folks had already taught us, were also an integral part of the curriculum at St. Philip's. You learned to speak only when spoken to, and to *always* formally address a nun as "Sister." This title often became slurred to "S'ter" in everyday spoken usage. It was much like the Marine Corps. A typical classroom answer might be: "*S'ter,* the capital of California is Sacramento, *S'ter.*" Or: "*S'ter,* a sacrament is an outward sign instituted by Christ to give grace, *S'ter.*"

Sister Osmond was probably the least intimidating and prettiest teacher I had at St. Philip's, that is if you can recognize beauty when only a face is visible, and not even a whole face. The voluminous and complex dress, or "habit," that the sisters wore covered almost everything, from the tops of their veiled and wimpled heads all the way to the floor and their usually invisible "sensible shoes," black lace-up oxfords. A nun's body was cloaked in mystery, not to mention yards of starched, folded, pinned and cinctured stark black and snowy white material. The headpiece allowed only the oval of the face to show, from mid-forehead to mid-chin. Even their ears were covered, and hair was nowhere in sight. (Many lay people assumed that nuns' heads were routinely shaved; that they had no hair. An early Sister-Superior at St. Philip's, Sister Liboria, was scandalized to accidentally overhear such nonsense on a parents' night, so she shocked everyone present by unpinning her headpiece and shaking out a full head of flowing red hair, putting that misconception to rest for good.) But young

Four St. Philip School teachers circa 1960.
L-R: Sisters Jolantha, Leonelle, Justin and Rose Sharon.

Sister Osmond was unmistakably pretty, and, like most of the first and second graders in her charge, I was smitten and half in love at the tender age of six.

Other than that forbidden and unrequited love for my teacher, I don't really remember much about those first couple of years at St. Philip's, aside from getting gold stick-on stars on my papers and saving our pennies for the "pagan babies." (And what was *that* all about anyway?) I guess I learned what I was supposed to, and must have been reasonably happy during that time. I met a lot of new kids, from town and from surrounding farms, and kids from Paris, Evart, Baldwin and Hersey.

From first through eighth grade we were seated alphabetically, so I was always in the desk behind Barbara Battle, a very smart and pretty girl, who provided me with stiff scholastic competition in every subject all the way through school. One of my best friends from first grade on was Keith Eichenberg, who, due to an as-yet undiscovered medical problem with his pituitary gland, was always rather undersized and puny, but he had a razor sharp wit and the small person's ability to turn aside bullies by using his sense of humor. Since I was always big for my age, we made a kind of Mutt and Jeff pair, but that was never a problem for us. And Keith was smart too, so there was a healthy competition for good grades always going on between us. Most importantly, however, I learned how great it was to have a best friend outside my own family, and we occasionally would go to each other's houses to play or spend the night. I remember that his mom always kept the linoleum floors in their house waxed and polished to a high gloss. You had to take your shoes off at Eichenbergs' place. The fun part of that was, when his Mom wasn't around, we would take turns sliding around on those shiny floors in our stocking feet, sometimes crashing into furniture or doors. Anyway, it was great having a friend like Keith.

My third and fourth grade teacher was Sister Justin. I think Sister Justin may have been at St. Philip's School from its beginning to its end, or around twenty years, for the school ceased operation as a Catholic school around 1970, at which time it was purchased by the Reed City Public School system to be used as additional classrooms and then later for administrative offices. Unlike Sister Osmond, Sister Justin could never be described as pretty. She was cursed with a couple of dark hairy moles on her face, kind of like old Witch Hazel in the *Little Lulu* comics we used to read back then, but she was a kind and effective teacher, and it was under her tutelage that I was first introduced to the mysteries and wonders of grammar, the parts of speech, and diagramming.

I could be wrong, but I don't think anyone diagrams sentences anymore, which is a real shame, because it helps you to understand how language works, not just your own language, but practically any language. I know, because I've studied a few foreign languages since Sister Justin first taught me about the various parts of speech and components of a sentence, and what I learned in the fourth grade has served me well all my life. I have always found the study of

Sister Mary Justin, SSND, circa 1960.

language, including English, to be quite fascinating. It was easy for me from the outset of studying grammar and the parts of speech to identify the nouns, verbs, adjectives, adverbs, prepositions or conjunctions. And figuring out where all these various parts and phrases of a sentence went in a diagram was more fun than any puzzle. Sister Justin would write sentences of varying and progressive complexity on the blackboard, and together we would break them down by form and function. I'll admit I was probably in the minority in my enthusiasm for grammar drills and sentence diagramming, but Sister Justin was a good enough teacher that just about everyone in her class was usually able to grasp the basic concepts.

At St. Philip's we continued to study grammar and diagram sentences right through the eighth grade. So it was a revelation to us Catholic school grammar geeks when we entered the public school system in ninth or tenth grade that most of the public school kids didn't know how to diagram a sentence. In fact, many of them didn't even know the difference between a noun and a verb, or a subject and a predicate. They'd never properly learned the simplest parts of speech that we had learned in the fourth grade, thanks to Sister Justin.

Spelling was another linguistic hat trick I excelled at. It just seemed to come naturally to me with a minimum amount of effort. I didn't even have to spend much time studying the assigned word lists, which Sister Justin assigned from the speller. We had almost daily spelling tests, usually twenty or thirty words each day. After Sister had carefully dictated the words, using each in a sentence and then repeating them, and we had written them down, we would trade papers and correct our tests. I could never become too cocky about my spelling and grammar tests though, because I usually traded papers with Barbara Battle, who always did as well as I did, and sometimes better. We also had "spelldowns" or "spelling bees." These were competitions in which we would line up across the front of the room or stand at our desks and Sister Justin would fire words at us to spell in succession. If you misspelled a word, you sat down and were eliminated from the competition. I usually made it to the final few, and often won (but so did Barbara). I had a lot of fun with my spelling skills a couple years later when, on the TV show *The $64,000 Question,* a child contestant's category was spelling. The final question, for the sixty-four grand, was to spell "antidisestablishmentarianism," which I (and a lot of other people too) thought was a little too easy.

While English was fun for me, math, or "arithmetic," as it was called then, was a horror, especially those darn "story problems." You know the kind I mean – "If a train leaves Chicago at 8AM, traveling at an average speed of 60 mph, blah-blah-blah." I just *hated* that stuff, and would usually zone out before the train ever left the station. This math aversion would follow me through out high school and college. I also had some initial trouble learning to tell time, a secret I managed to keep into the fourth grade, and, when I saw "time problems" coming up in our arithmetic book, I would often manage to stay home "sick" that day. But this didn't work for long. Mom found out what my problem was, and set me down one of those "sick" afternoons with a clock, and, probably in a half hour or so, taught me how to tell time.

Straight arithmetic problems involving just numbers –

addition, subtraction, multiplication and division long and short – I didn't have any problems with. Sister Justin spent time every day drilling the class in the "times tables." We were required to memorize all the multiplication tables from twos through twelves, and would daily drone aloud through sets of tables, all together now: "Four times four is sixteen. Four times five is twenty. Four times six is twenty-four," ad nauseam, until our times tables became as familiar to us as our own names.

But life at St. Philip's School wasn't *all* work and study. There was also recess and lunch time, probably the favorite subjects of many kids, then *and* now. We had a reasonably well-equipped playground, with swings, see-saws (we called them "teeter-totters"), and a merry-go-round, all situated in a gravel-covered play area. (I never have figured out why play areas were paved or gravel covered. Either surface can be pretty hard on little knees and elbows when you fell or got pushed down.) This equipment was used mostly by the youngest kids. By the time you reached fourth or fifth grade, there were more challenging things to do. The girls did a lot of rope-skipping and whatever else girls that age do. The boys were into playing marbles, or more physical games like Red Rover (aka "pom-pom-pullaway") or "King of the Hill."

Sometimes these rougher games got a bit out of hand, particularly if we were far enough out on the playground so the Sisters couldn't easily see us. We played King of the Hill on a dirt and gravel partially grassed-over hummock out behind the backstop to the softball field. It was actually a little beyond the playground and outside the playing fields proper, which is probably what made it so attractive to boys who were testing their own strength and the limits of the rules. I remember one particular game in which Jack Hurst and I had formed a spontaneous alliance to hold the top of the hill, and were successfully fending off all attempts at incursion, pushing and flinging the other boys off in all directions. Unfortunately, things must have gotten a bit too physical when we forcibly threw down one of the smaller boys, Billy Lehman, who landed awkwardly at the foot of the hill and began to cry, something that would normally have brought immediate scorn and taunts of "crybaby," but we all saw at once how one of his arms was bent unnaturally underneath him. The game ceased at once and we all gathered around him, glancing fearfully back at the

1955 (age 11)

playground for the Sisters, already mentally formulating our "We were just *playing*, S'ter!" excuses.

As it turned out, Billy had to be taken to the hospital for a compound fracture of his right arm, which was duly set and put into a heavy, L-shaped plaster cast, which enveloped his scrawny little arm from shoulder to wrist and was supported by a sling. When he returned to school sporting this impressive apparatus a couple days later, he became a kind of instant celebrity, with all the kids clamoring to sign his cast and carry his books or lunch tray. I was probably the most fervently eager to be his lackey, since I felt deeply guilty and ashamed of my part in his injury. Of course, Jack and I were both in the doghouse with the Sisters for our oafish, savage behavior, and King of the Hill was pretty much banned forever. If there was anything good that came out of this incident, it was that Jack and I became pretty close friends from then on. We savage oafs had to stick together.

Lunch period was, as I said, a pretty popular subject at St. Philip's. Not the least reason for this was the good, homemade hot lunches served up by Mr. and Mrs. Morris. Florence Morris was the combination cook-and-lunchlady at St. Philip's, and also sometimes filled in for the nuns as a spelling or religion teacher. Fred Morris was the custodian for both the church and the school and sometimes cook's helper too. At times Fred would need a hand with some of the heavier chores around the school and the older boys vied for the "privilege" of working with Mr. Morris. As a matter of fact, one summer (I think it was between seventh and eighth grades) I had the honor of working a couple weeks with Mr. Morris, helping him to strip, scrub and wax the tile floors throughout the school. I didn't know at the time what valuable lessons I was learning when Fred taught me how to operate the electric floor scrubber-buffer, a job that's not as easy as it looks. It was a skill I made good use of later on, first in the Army, and then in a part-time custodial job that helped put me through college. Fred was a good teacher, patient and encouraging, and I loved working with him. He made me feel important.

But, getting back to recess and my "bully days" in the fourth grade, while I was really never a bully, I was always one of the biggest kids in my class, and not just tall either. I was on the chubby side, to be perfectly frank. I couldn't wear regular kid size jeans, or "overalls," as we called them then. My mother had to order a special cut of jeans from Sears and Roebuch called "Huskies," much to my chagrin. These "special" pants did not escape the attention of my classmates, and some of the crueler boys would often taunt me about my size. I spent a lot of my recesses chasing an Evart kid named Kenny Lipe, who used to call me "Two-ton Tony." Or sometimes he and other kids would chant an old advertising slogan at me: "Fatty, Fatty, run for your life. Here comes Skinny with an Oleson Knife." Usually I couldn't catch Kenny, but when I did, I would hold him down by sitting on his chest, a real Two-ton Tony tactic if there ever was one. Thankfully, my fat phase only lasted a few years, until sixth grade, when I underwent a sudden growth spurt and lost most of the offending baby fat.

My teacher for the fifth and sixth grades was Sister Mary James, whom I remember most for her encouraging me as an "artist," which was probably more a kindness than evidence of any real talent on my part. But I did like to draw, and spent a lot of time trying to draw horses, as I was in the middle of my *Black Stallion* and other horse stories reading phase. I also engaged in a project where I drew portraits of all the presidents, which I copied freehand from a book about the presidents. Sister James displayed these on the hall bulletin boards for all the students to see, which pleased me enormously.

We also spent a lot of time on history and geography those two years, and memorizing all the state capitals and world capitals, many of which I can still remember. Rote memorization and group classroom drills *do* work. I (and my whole generation) are living proof of it.

There was also a great deal of memorization involved in what passed for religion class in these grades. We were covering the last parts of *The Baltimore Catechism*, in preparation for receiving the

sacrament of Confirmation. This sacrament was really a big deal, kind of the Catholic or Christian equivalent of the Jewish bar mitzvah ritual, which celebrates the beginning of adulthood and religious responsibility. It was usually conferred sometime between the ages of twelve and fourteen, or whenever the Bishop could make the trip from Grand Rapids to our parish. In preparation for this holy event, we memorized whole sections of questions and answers from the catechism. We also had to pick a new Confirmation name (I picked John) and needed an adult sponsor. Our family friend, Albert Rohe (Fred's dad) did the honors for me, standing behind me with a hand on my shoulder while the Bishop annointed me with the holy oils that officially made me a "soldier of Christ." Confirmation was an official rite of passage, a coming of age in the Church, and Sister James never missed an opportunity to remind us of this, and to urge us to behave like "ladies and gentlemen."

Of course, by sixth grade there were other more obvious reasons for importuning polite behavior and attempting to inculcate basic social graces. Hormones were just beginning to stir. The differences between boys and girls were starting to show.

Sin, Social Graces, Music
and Religious Vocations

How do you address the matter of your own budding sexuality in a memoir you hope your children will read? It presents a dilemma, but, in the interest of honesty, you can't simply gloss over it, because, beginning with pre-adolescence and on into adulthood, sex becomes a driving force and often, for a time at least, an all-consuming obsession. So, here's the way I remember it.

When I was about twelve years old, my dick developed a will all its own. Sex raised its ugly head. Certain female images – a glimpse of a breast, the dark mystery of "cleavage," a stray visible lingerie strap – could cause an immediate and often embarrassing erection. And hey, I didn't even know what an erection *was* when all this started. The word wasn't even a part of my vocabulary. The closest thing to it would have been the Erector Set my brother Rich had, which was a collection of miniature metal girders and beams, and nuts, bolts and screws to fasten them together to build little skyscrapers and derricks and suchlike. Anyway, these early erections were really a source of confusion and wonder to me. No one had ever talked to me about sex, so I was pretty much on my own.

Interestingly enough however, it was about this same time that our catechism lessons began to dwell on the subject of "purity" and "*im*-purity," and how we must strive to avoid impure thoughts and "occasions of sin." Ah-*ha*! These "thoughts" I'd been having, and the erratic behavior of my friend "Dick" must somehow be related to impurity and *SIN*! And, being a good Catholic boy, I knew that sin was to be avoided at all cost. Sin was *EVIL*! Sin was *BAD*! Sin made God sad and disappointed in us. Unfortunately, by the time I'd made this connection, the damage was already done. I had discovered, quite by accident, the excitement and exquisite sensations of masturbation – yet another word that was not yet in my vocabulary, but whatever you called it, it sure felt *GOOD*!

The first actual name for this activity I got from a priest in the confessional, for, like the nuns who were harping on the virtues of purity and self-control in religion classes, the priests were also obviously fine-tuned to the incipient concupiscence of pre-adolescent boys. (Well, why not? They were boys once too, right?) So it was right about this time, when I first hesitatingly confessed to having "impure thoughts," that the priest began questioning me further along these lines. "And when you have these impure thoughts, do you *touch* yourself?" Blushing furiously, and thankful to the very tips of my toes for the darkness and anonymity of the confessional (Ha! Anonymity my ass! Father Cusack or Gallagher knew perfectly well who I was), I would mumble, "Yes, Father." The priest would then patiently explain that "self abuse" was a *mortal* sin, and was to be assiduously avoided. Well, he didn't say "assiduously," but he made it pretty damn clear that I'd better stop it, or I would go to Hell, literally.

So two things happened here. First, I finally had a name to pin on this awful, terrible, wonderful, terrific thing I was doing – "self abuse." (Hmm ... seems somehow inadequate, especially in retrospect.) Second, I learned about guilt, especially "Catholic guilt," something that would haunt me for years to come. I mean, let's face it. You don't just quit doing something that feels that *good*, no matter how *bad* the priests and nuns tell you it is. But here was the real problem: it was a *mortal* sin. Mortal sins are the really serious ones – the ones that can damn you to the fires of Hell for all eternity. Not like piddling little "venial" sins that can be paid off by saying a few Hail Marys. So what's a kid to do when he's hopelessly addicted to this one particular mortal sin? Do you realize how scary it was for the next several years for me, knowing that I was almost constantly in a state of mortal sin, and that if I got hit by a car and killed I'd go straight to Hell? Yes, straight to HELL; no appeals or pardons, and no short sentence in Purgatory, but straight to HELL! Do not pass Go, and do not collect two hundred dollars. Proceed directly to HELL! Being killed while in a state of mortal sin was kind of the spiritual equivalent of being killed while wearing dirty underwear. Your mother would be absolutely mortified.

No wonder then, that I ran to confession every Saturday for years, hoping I'd get there safely, to have my sullied soul once again washed clean by the priest's absolution, prayers of penance and a "firm purpose of amendment" (which often did not last past Sunday night). And those "occasions of sin" I was to avoid were everywhere, and so easy to find, from magazine advertisements ("I dreamed I was a princess in my Maidenform Bra"), to previews or billboards of movies starring Sophia Loren, Gina Lolobrigida or Anita Ekberg (their films were usually condemned by the Catholic Legion of Decency), or even the innocent (to everyone *else*) lingerie sections of the staid Sears and Roebuck or Montgomery Ward catalogues. Literally *everything* was a near occasion of sin for me, and, to make things even worse, I was sure that I was the only one who did these despicable things.

Years later, reading Philip Roth's bestselling novel, *Portnoy's Complaint*, I knew exactly what young Alex Portnoy meant when he said he was whacking off so much and so often that he lived in dread of reaching the point where he would begin to "come blood." Sometimes the compulsion was just overwhelming – any random erotic thought or the slightest bit of accidental friction would set me off and send me running for refuge behind a closed door to relieve the pressure, or re-live the pleasure – or both.

If it hadn't been for all that Catholic guilt, I suppose it could have been a pretty wonderful thing, this sexual awakening that comes to everyone. But instead it was an absolutely miserable time of my life. I spent much of my time worrying about dying in this horrible state of mortal sin. On the other hand, however, once I'd broken that not-so-firm purpose of amendment after a blessed twenty-four hours or less of being in a "state of grace" following confession, I figured, what the hell, I'm already damned, I might as get in as many whacks as possible before confessions again next Saturday. In short, in spite of all the teachings of Holy Mother

Church, it was no contest. Hormones always won out over grace and holiness.

Having said all this, I think I should emphasize that I don't mean to make light of the matter of early sexuality and the problems that children (and their parents) have with it. Quite the contrary. I recognize – I *remember* in excruciatingly vivid detail – what a terrible time those years can be for a kid. Maybe if someone had just sat down and talked with me about sex and what was happening to me, some of the misery and awful guilt of those years could have been avoided. But that kind of candor just wasn't available in those days, at least certainly not within the confines of the teachings of the Catholic Church. It was a sin, and a *mortal* sin. Period.

Many years later, as an adult, I talked about this with a priest, and told him that I just couldn't view things like "impure thoughts," or even masturbation, as serious sins anymore. In fact, they barely seemed worth mentioning, especially when you considered all the terrible things people did to themselves and each other that did serious harm – sins of anger and physical violence and hate. The priest's advice was simple, and a bit startling. He told me, "If something no longer feels like a sin, then it probably isn't." This was in the eighties. I'm still a little puzzled by his answer. Do standards of sin or thresholds of seriousness change and evolve like people do? Apparently so. Or perhaps the Church itself has evolved into a "kinder, gentler" arbiter. At any rate, I certainly could have used some of that kindness when I was thirteen or fourteen years old.

Interestingly enough (thank God), this "dark side" of my sexual development never spilled over (no pun intended) into my interpersonal relations with girls of my own age at this time. I was simultaneously going through on-and-off crushes and cases of unrequited puppy love for various girls at school. I was especially infatuated with Maureen Milligan, a new girl who joined our class in the sixth grade when her family moved to Reed City. She had long dark brown hair, soft brown eyes, and a demure manner and soft-spokenness that just about undid me at the age of twelve. I was pretty smitten with her for the next couple of years, but mostly too shy to do much about it, at least publicly. That year when we exchanged school pictures with all our classmates, I took

Maureen's wallet-size photo to the local photographer, Mr. Earp, and had him make me an 8X10 copy, which I framed and set on the chest of drawers in the room I shared with Bob. I took some nasty ribbing from Bob about that initially, but he got over it. (Well, maybe not. More on that later.) Although I did a lot of fruitless mooning over Maureen during this period, I did notice other girls too, as there were some attractive girls around, like Sherry Finnerty, a cute, flirtatious honey blonde from Baldwin, or Jenny Bayak, another Baldwin girl, brown-eyed and brunette, who acted a bit older than the rest of us and was perhaps a bit sexually precocious, but *I* certainly never found out. When I did notice or pay attention to these other girls, I would feel vaguely unfaithful to Maureen, which was pretty ridiculous, since I was never able to articulate my feelings to her anyway. In short, I was the usual welter of hormonal confusion and klutziness that most adolescent boys are.

When we were in the seventh grade, St. Philip's School made a Friday field trip to Grand Rapids to attend the Shrine Circus. We were bused to Baldwin, where we took the train to Grand Rapids. The train ride was a first for most of the students. In many ways that short train trip was more exciting than the circus itself. There was a kind of mini-scandal that followed that trip, because the nuns got wind of some boy-girl pairing off that had supposedly taken place on the train ride back to Baldwin. Well, of course some kids did pair up on the train, but I don't think anything much happened. Perhaps a couple of kisses got sneaked, I don't know. I think I may have gotten a little seat time with Maureen on that return trip, but we probably spent most of that time playing with my lizard. Wait, that's not as bad as it might sound. I had bought a small chameleon in a little cardboard box at the circus. We were fascinated by how it changed colors to match its perch or surroundings, so we were experimenting with that during the ride home. (Apparently too much handling was not healthy for the little lizard, because it died the next day.) At any rate, the following Monday Sister Mildred, our teacher, held a mini-inquisition, taking all the seventh-and eighth-grade girls individually into the office to be interrogated about their activities on the train, and whether there had been any nastiness involving the boys. Like I said, I doubt that there was, but the good Sisters were ever vigilant.

Seventh and eighth grades kind of run together in my memory. Our teacher was Sister Mary Mildred, a mostly good-humored, red-faced blustery sort, who made allowances for the boisterous vulgarity that teenage boys are often prone to. We always felt pretty fortunate to have Sister Mildred as our teacher then, because the previous teacher for grades seven and eight had been much less tolerant. Sister Gaudentia had had very little patience for the farm-boy humor of some of her students, who used to risk getting their knuckles rapped with a ruler just to get her going. She abhorred any sort of scatological humor or bodily noises, and it seemed her favorite phrase was, "Who made that nasty noise in their throat?" So, just to set her off, one of the boys in the back of the room would belch loudly, sending her bustling back to rap him a good one. Then a crony in the front of the room would burp, and she'd hustle up there to crack that one. Then, as the coup de gras, someone in the back would rip off a loud fart, and, when she *still* said, "Who made that nasty noise in their throat?" it would set everyone off in a gale of giggles and guffaws. Great fun for the class, but probably not for poor, high-strung Sister Gaudentia.

But our Sister Mildred was an entirely different story. One of the extraordinary things she taught us was how to dance. I guess she figured that at our ages, it was time to learn some social graces. So, on rainy days or frigid winter ones, we would push all our desks back against the walls, get out the phonograph and records, and she would instruct us in the dance. We started out with square dancing, learning the niceties of bow to your partner, alemande left, do-si-do, and the promenade. When we screwed up, Sister would stop the record and walk us through the moves until we got it right. Then we moved on to the one-two-three rhythms of the polka, with many stepped-on toes and much dizzy lurching into the desks and each other. Finally she taught us the box step of the waltz, no doubt after much soul-searching, for this kind of slow dancing could probably be considered a much "near-er" occasion of sin than the faster steps, what with all the hand holding and touching required (although emphasis was placed on keeping a proper space between dance partners). Of course most all the girls loved these days of learning to dance. For many of the boys, however, it was sheer torture. I remember poor Raymond Battle, in particular, making a couple clumsy attempts at waltzing, and then, finally, flatly refusing to participate anymore, chin jutting defiantly.

Sister Mildred gently tried to cajole him back, reasoning, "Raymond, if you don't know how to dance, how do you ever expect to get a girl to marry you?"

"I ain't never gettin' married!" Raymond replied hotly.

"You *aren't* ever getting married," Sister corrected.

"That's *right*!" said Raymond emphatically, and that concluded his short-lived education in the social graces.

My own reaction to dancing was quite different. Although I could never be accused of being graceful, I did enjoy the chance to actually touch and hold a real live girl under socially acceptable circumstances, and I did have a reasonably good sense of rhythm, and enjoyed the music.

Music had always enjoyed a prominent place in our family life. My mom told me that when she and Dad were first married and money was tight, she would often use a part of the money they budgeted for entertainment to buy records, which, unlike a dinner or a movie, could be enjoyed over and over again. Because of Mom's love for music (Dad was rather indifferent to music), we grew up in a music-filled home. Whenever Mom was home with us kids, either the radio or the record player was usually turned on. Our first records were the heavy but fragile wax 78 rpm discs of the time. We had a pretty sizeable collection of these by the time I began to really take notice of music, in the early fifties. We listened to Bing Crosby and the Andrews Sisters, Perry Como, Tennessee Ernie Ford, Rusty Draper, Guy Lombardo, Guy Mittchell, Lawrence Welk, Wee Bonnie Baker, Julius LaRosa, Eddie Fisher – in short, most of the popular music makers of the era.

To this day, I can still sing along with some of the novelty tunes of that time, mostly long-forgotten by everyone else; songs like, "I'm a Lonely Little Petunia in an Onion Patch (and all I do is cry all day)," by Dick "Two-Ton" Baker, or Jimmy Boyd's "I'm Gettin' Nuttin' for Christmas," or PeeWee King's "Slowpoke" (admirably covered by the old redhead Arthur Godfrey in his trademark adenoidal croak). And on car trips our whole family would sing "Goodnight, Irene," a folk tune made popular by the Weavers.

The accordion was a popular instrument of the early fifties, championed not just by Lawrence Welk and his protege, Myron

Floren, but also by Frankie Yankovic and Dick Contino. It was also an integral part of many western swing bands and could be heard on the records of Gene Autry and Roy Rogers.

Apparently hoping for a musician in the family, Mom got Dad to buy a small twelve-bass accordion (and later on a big 120-bass) and sent us four older boys (and later Mary) to a local musician of some renown, Eddie Kutzbach, to take lessons. I didn't last long at this, as he tried to teach us to read music, something I never learned, but managed to fake it for a few months by learning my practice pieces by ear and memorizing them. I don't think any of us stayed with the accordion for very long, except my sister Mary, who can still play some and has even given lessons herself. And my brother Bill can still noodle on it some, but Bill may be the most natural musician in our family. He taught himself to play the guitar and the banjo, after a fashion, while he was in college, somewhat to the detriment of his studies, since his budding musicianship added an extra year or so to his college time.

So although I wasn't a musician, I *was* a music lover, and I came of age musically around the time of the birth of modern rock and roll. When I was twelve, Elvis burst upon the music scene like a meteor. Our family gathered in front of the TV every Saturday night to watch *Your Hit Parade*, which presented the top ten songs of the past week, along with a couple of "extras." There were several weeks in 1956 when Elvis had three songs in the top ten: "Hound Dog," "Don't Be Cruel," and "Heartbreak Hotel." My brother Rich had all of these songs on 45 rpm records, and I used to sneakily borrow them whenever he wasn't around and play them over and over again on our small Zenith radio-phonograph in the living room, rocking and bopping and singing along, like a million other teenagers of the time. I probably just about drove my mom nuts, but she never complained.

At around this time, age twelve or thirteen, I began buying and collecting records myself, mostly 45s at first, until I started working for my dad at the elevator and could start to afford the more pricey LPs. My first purchased 45 was a Johnny Ray song, "Just Walking in the Rain," followed soon after by Marty Robbins' "A White Sport Coat (and a Pink Carnation)." Many others followed in quick succession, whenever I could scrape together a dollar or so. There was Buddy Holly, Roy Orbison, Johnny Cash,

The Everly Brothers, Johnny Burnette, Bobby Vee, Ferlin Husky, LeRoy Van Dyke, Stonewall Jackson (there was a lot of country-pop crossover then), and countless others, including, of course, everything Elvis.

To me, Elvis was the epitome of cool, with his half-sneer smile, turned-up collar, and greased-back hair, called, variously (for those who don't remember), a ducktail, a duck's ass, or DA. How I *wanted* hair like that, and how I tried to cultivate it. Alas, my dad wouldn't allow it. Every time the hair on the sides of my head got almost long enough to comb back in that graceful greasy sweep, it was off to the barber with me, and I *better* get the usual conservative whitewall-style cut too, or I'd go right back to the shop and would have to pay for the second cut myself. So I used up a lot of Vitalis and Vaseline hair tonic trying to train my meager sidewalls to comb *back*, straining toward that elusive DA, so I could properly emulate my idol.

Elvis remained my model of choice for a year or two, and my first-ever album purchase was his *Christmas Album*, which featured several pages of glossy color photos of Elvis. The original edition of this album, in pristine condition, is today a much sought-after and valuable collector's item. Unfortunately, my copy was played half to death in those first years, so was pretty worn. And my brother Bob (remember him?), no Elvis fan, for mysterious reasons known only to him, defaced most of the photos by blacking out teeth or drawing moustaches on them, making the album totally worthless – except to me.

Around the age of fourteen, I switched my musical allegiance from Elvis (although I always remained a loyal fan) to Ricky Nelson, who was a bit closer to my own age, still just a kid himself, really. Oddly enough, I became a fan based solely on Rick's musical efforts, for I had never seen the Ozzie and Harriet TV show, where Rick co-starred with his parents and his older brother David. (They also had a radio show before that, but I never heard it either.) Television reception was limited and iffy where we lived, and the Nelson family show was not on either of the two channels we could receive with any clarity. But I identified with Rick's records from the very start, as did millions of other kids all over the country. His first single's A-side, released when he was just sixteen, was a cover of Fats Domino's "I'm Walkin'," which I loved bopping along with, but I think I understood the flip side even better, a sappy, teen-angst ballad called, "A Teenager's Romance." Critics dismissed it as hack-written dreck, but dammit, I *still* like it.

I'm digressing, I know, I know. Where was I? Oh yeah, Sister Mildred and dancing. Since Sister Mildred established a kind of precedent by bringing music into the classroom when we were learning to dance, it wasn't too difficult, by the time I was in the eighth grade, to persuade her to let us bring *our* records to school to swap and play at recess and lunch hour on bad weather days. This became a pretty popular socialization activity that last year at St. Philip's, when we were the elite upperclassmen. It even spilled over a little into after-school stuff. I remember one blissful and awkward afternoon when I shared a couple records with Maureen at her house. I think they were probably Tab Hunter's version of "Young Love" and "Why Don't They Understand," by George Hamilton IV. When you're only thirteen or fourteen, sappy love lyrics can seem excruciatingly real.

That last year at St. Philip's was a pivotal one for me – a transition, from my rather sheltered, limited life thus far, to a new kind of experience, because the following year, 1958, I was to leave home for boarding school, at St. Joseph's Seminary in Grand Rapids.

This "decision" on my part was not such an abrupt surprise as it might seem. To even call it a decision would hardly be accurate. This was still the fifties, an era when Catholic schools still flourished throughout Michigan and throughout the country. These schools were often used by the Church as training grounds for potential candidates for the religious life. There were constant subtle (and not-so-subtle) urgings in that direction by both the nuns or brothers who taught in these schools and by the parish priests, who enjoyed positions of enormous respect and power in those days within their communities. So if after several years of daily Mass, force-fed religion classes, and close contact with priests through serving as an altar boy, your pastor and your teachers began suggesting you could very well have a "vocation" to the priesthood, you listened, and began to think seriously about it. When you're only thirteen or fourteen years old you can be pretty easily influenced, especially if you've spent most of your life trying your best to be a "good Catholic boy."

St. Philip School
Reed City, Michigan

Father (later Monsignor) Victor P. Gallagher,
pastor at St. Philip (May 1962).

Eighth Grade diploma.

I already knew a couple other older boys from the parish, brothers Bob and Delvin Tilman, who were attending St. Joseph's. And to top it all off, my brother Bob had already spent a couple years there, so Mom and Dad figured at least if I did decide to go, I wouldn't be "all alone" – Bob would be there too. As it turned out, after I'd made my decision to go, and all the paperwork and a physical exam and and other preparations had been made, at the very last minute, the last week before classes were to begin, Bob decided he would not return to the seminary, but would go to Reed City High instead. But even then I was not to go off to Grand Rapids by myself. My best friend, Keith Eichenberg, decided to go too.

I should probably note here that I was not really an "easy sell" on the idea of studying for the priesthood. First, the idea of celibacy wasn't all that appealing to me, even at that young age. I liked girls. (I didn't just *like* them; I was *fascinated* by them.) Second, I was still plagued by the "purity" issue and was "abusing" myself at every opportunity, in spite of a shitload of good intentions. Even to my adolescent mind, this seemed to make me pretty poor priest material. However, by this time, after a few years of struggling to

The boys of St. Philip School graduating class, 1958. L-R: Tim Bazzett, Keith Eichenberg, Jack Hurst, Leon Saladin, Eugene Kailing, Lewis Duffing.

keep my hands off myself, I knew that both our parish priests, Fathers Gallagher and Cusack, knew all about my particular problems through the confessional (which really isn't all that "anonymous" in a small parish). They both assured me I was an "excellent candidate." Even their assurances might not have persuaded me, as I still harbored a major crush on Maureen. But Sister Mildred took care of that. One day, while asking me if I'd made up my mind about the seminary, she told me confidentially that she knew I had "special feelings" for Maureen, but then assured me that she was pretty sure that Maureen had plans to enter the convent (to become a nun). Now I don't know if Sister Mildred was telling an outright lie (albeit for the greater good and glory of Christ Jesus) in order to clinch my recruitment, or if Maureen actually was considering a religious vocation at the time, but it had the effect of finally bursting my romantic adolescent bubble, and helped me over the hump to make that decision. I would be a good Catholic boy and give it a go.

Maureen, by the way, never entered the convent. She began dating my brother Bob in high school. When I came home from the seminary on vacation and found this out, I found that 8X10 framed photo I had kept of her in my bureau drawer, took it out behind the house one night and buried it in the garbage pit. Several years later Maureen and Bob married and ended up having *seven* kids. (Thank you, Sister Mildred. I know I thought I loved her, but I don't think I loved her *that* much.)

St. Joseph Seminary:
Prayer, Study and Wet Dreams

My memories of St. Joseph Seminary are, at best, rather vague and fragmented. Initially it was very difficult for me to adjust. It was my first experience with living away from home and I was dreadfully homesick. I missed my parents and I missed being able to just walk into town whenever I wanted. I missed Reed City. I missed my room. I missed the *privacy* of my room.

The first-year freshmen at St. Joseph's were all housed in an enormous barrack-like room on the third floor of the main building, with a high ceiling and tall windows all around. We slept in Army-style metal bunk beds and kept our clothes in metal lockers. The floor was, I think, highly waxed and polished linoleum. There was a large communal bathroom right outside the dormitory with rows of sinks, urinals and toilet stalls. In this setting, privacy was a scarce commodity.

Our lives were extremely regimented, and revolved around the dual disciplines of prayer and study. We rose early, around six, I think, and went directly to chapel for morning prayers, then to breakfast in the communal "refectory." Then there was a steady round of classes, study hall, and recreation time, punctuated by still more prayers in chapel at noon, in the late afternoon and again in the evening. Many of our prayers and most of the hymns we sang were in Latin. We were all issued a heavy black book containing all these prayers and hymns, called the *Liber Usualis*. Prayer and chapel were the overriding constants in seminary life. Every student had his assigned place and pew – no slouching, no dozing, and when it was time to kneel, it was back straight, head up, no butt touching the seat.

The grounds of St. Joseph took up an entire city block at 600 Burton Street. As I remember it, there were three buildings. The largest main building held the administration office, classrooms and study hall, a library, dormitories for grades nine through twelve, student lounge and auditorium, kitchen and refectory, some faculty living quarters, a barber shop and postal room, and, of course, at its heart, the chapel.

A second newer building held rooms for the upperclassmen, who were in the first two years of college, along with some more faculty quarters. I can't remember ever going into this building. I'm not sure, but I think there was a kind of unspoken rule that underclassmen were not permitted in the college dormitory. There were probably good reasons for this "rule," one being to avoid the possibility of any "special friendships" being formed between the older students and the younger ones. Another reason for this separation was that the college-age students enjoyed a rather exalted status at St. Joseph's, a school where the attrition rate each succeeding year could be very high. If you made it through the first four years then your "vocation" was considered to be a very strong one.

The third building on campus, also a newer one, was the gymnasium, which held a good-sized basketball court and a few indoor handball courts. Handball, usually a big city sport, was brand new to me, as it was to most incoming freshmen, but it was a phys ed staple at any seminary. All it requires is a wall and a ball. It's a little like tennis, except the two opponents are side by side, and play the ball, a small, palm-size hard rubber one, off the wall in front of them, on an outside court. On an inside court, there are three walls to contend with. I never became particularly good at handball, but did play it casually during my time at St. Joe's, as did almost everyone there, including the faculty priests.

Physical education and sports were an integral part of the curriculum at St. Joe's – a healthy mind in a healthy body – and, indeed, the remainder of the grounds at the the seminary were taken up by playing fields, used for football (touch only), baseball, softball, tennis, and track and field events. In the wintertime, one of these fields was usually flooded and frozen to make a large skating rink.

Everyone was strongly encouraged to participate in sports year-round. At high-school level there were no league competitions with other area schools. Our sports were strictly intramural. I played some softball, a little football, learned a little about basketball in some pick-up games, and ran some track. And, of course, I played handball, which, although it could be a fiercely competitive and physical sport, also served as a kind of socialization tool. The opponents, usually friends, could visit and goof off while playing at handball.

But obviously it wasn't all play at St. Joe's. A tremendous emphasis was placed on academics and study. The faculty at the seminary enforced the same maxim that my dad had always pushed: Work *first. Then* play.

The school week at St. Joe's had one oddity, but one which I quickly adapted to and even grew to like. There were classes and study hall periods for a half-day on Saturday mornings. But, to compensate for this, Wednesday afternoons were free for recreation, sports and leisure time. This provided a welcome mid-week respite from the daily grind of study and classes.

One of the most common forms of recreation or of filling leisure time was walking the perimeter. As I've mentioned, the school grounds took up a whole city block. Three sides of the block were enclosed by a six-foot chain link security fence and closely-spaced trees and shrubs growing all along the fence-line. We used to joke about what it was like "on the outside." It's true we weren't prisoners, but at times it would feel that way, particularly to the boys who came from outside of Grand Rapids, and couldn't get back home unassisted even if they wanted to. It took maybe ten or fifteen minutes to circle our block, and sometimes we'd follow that path several times a day. Often we underclassmen would spend much of those walks keeping a sharp eye out for girls walking outside the fence. In addition, many close friendships were forged during those daily perimeter walks, where we got to know each other and shared memories and childhood experiences.

A couple of my closest friends made that year were two pals from the same Grand Rapids parish, Tom Cassleman, whose desk adjoined mine in study hall, and his friend, Mike Gardner. Tom was a lean, athletic, intense kid, with a devilish sense of humor that often got him in hot water. Mike was just the opposite, being short, pudgy and definitely not very athletic, but also possessing a quiet sense of humor. He was the perfect foil for Tom, and sometimes for me too. We made that perimeter walk often, and bonded through silly activities such as staging mock fist fights, or creating reverse-spelling alter egos for ourselves and other classmates and faculty. Hence I was Mit Ttezzab and Tom was Mot Namelssac. We talked of books and pop music and even about girls – a frowned-upon subject, of course, given the seminary environment.

But girls and sex could not be completely expunged from the lives and thoughts of fourteen and fifteen year-old boys just because they were suddenly seminarians. No, the spectre of sex and the struggle against impure thoughts was still a problem for me, and, I suspect, for most of the boys at St. Joe's. Because of the communal living aspect and lack of privacy though, it was much more difficult to engage in the sinful solitary sex I had become so addicted to in the past couple of years. It wasn't impossible; it just required more ingenuity and imagination. True, the "occasions of sin" were much scarcer. There were, of course, no live girls or women around to be tempted by, and our TV and film watching was extremely limited due to rules and our full schedule of study, prayer, and recreation. There was little or nothing in the very carefully selected books of our library to inflame the sexual imagination of a teenage boy. (There were many very *good* books to read there, however. That year I remember reading, for example, James Fenimore Cooper's *The Deerslayer*, Marjorie Kinnan Rawlings' *The Yearling*, and Conrad Richter's *The Light in the Forest*.) We were encouraged to read some religious texts in our free time too. I chose to delve into *Lives of the Saints*, which offered short biographies of all the major and minor saints of the Church. Particularly fascinating were the tales of early martyrs and the gruesome tortures and executions they endured for refusing to renounce their faith. And it was here I managed to find some pretty tittilating narratives about virgin martyrs. My favorite was St. Agatha, who had both her breasts cut off and put on a plate – a grisly image, but, I'm ashamed to admit, in that particular setting of my life, one that I managed to find arousing. So yes, there were "occasions of sin" even in the so-called sacred writings, if you were ripe for sin and the hormones were high and raging.

On the other hand, I worked harder at maintaining my personal purity that year than ever before. I prayed hard about it, and successfully managed to keep my hands off myself much of the time. As a result of this, I began to experience erotic and embarrassing "wet dreams" at night in my bunk. Now no one had ever explained "nocturnal emissions" to me as a natural phenomenon, so the first few times this happened to me I was rather horrified. I thought I'd wet the bed when I awoke to damp sticky sheets and underwear, and was terribly afraid of being found out and ridiculed for my baby-ish regression. This would sometimes happen two or three times a week, and I soon realized, by a combination of intuition and hearing other older boys joking about wet dreams and morning "boners," what was happening. (Hey, when you keep manufacturing the stuff, it's got to get out somehow.) Nevertheless, I continued to be secretly embarrassed by this quite natural occurrence, and carefully folded or wadded my sheets on linen-changing days to try to conceal the semen stains (or "pecker tracks," as we later learned to matter-of-factly call them) when I turned them in at the laundry.

Our personal laundry – clothing, towels and washcloths – did not get washed at the seminary. Everyone had a heavy-duty cardboard laundry box, or "kit," and every week or two we would pack all our soiled clothing into this box and take it to the basement mail-room to send it home for our moms to wash. I don't know what Mom thought about all those stained and crusty jockey shorts, but, since I was the fourth boy in the family, I suppose it wasn't anything new to her. But it did provide me with one more embarrassing secret shame.

No one much enjoyed packing and sending out those laundry kits, but getting them back by return mail was another story and often a cause for celebration, since not only did you get a supply of clean, fresh-smelling clothes, but you'd also often get a contraband stash of homemade cookies or brownies or maybe some candy. Some kids hoarded this stuff in their lockers. I generally shared it with my friends and it was quickly gone.

Sharing these treats from home was not really any great sacrifice, as we were very well fed every day. Meals were prepared by an order of nuns, who labored long hours in the seminary kitchen every day and prepared large scrumptious meals that were about as close to home-cooking as you could get. Bread was baked fresh every day, and the aroma of this baking bread never failed to make my mouth water whenever I would pass by the kitchen. On Sundays we were treated to homemade frosted raisin bread, which was truly "to die for," as the saying goes.

Meals were taken largely in silence, if you can imagine a couple hundred boys and young men eating quietly. There were ten to twelve boys seated at each table, including a prefect to keep order, and two boys who would act as servers, bringing the dishes of food and pitchers of milk or other drinks to the table. Only minimal necessary talk was permitted, such as asking for food to be passed. There was, however, plenty of mental stimulation provided at each meal – food for the mind, if you will. An upperclassman reader was appointed, usually on a weekly basis, and, once the food had been blessed, he would read to us while we dined. Sometimes the selection would be of a religious nature, but more often than not it would be from an "approved" popular book of the time. The one book I can remember being read from beginning to end over an extended period of time was *The Day Lincoln Was Shot*, by Jim Bishop, which everyone seemed to enjoy immensely – and got an in-depth history lesson at the same time.

Academics were always a primary emphasis at St. Joe's. Incoming freshmen were always kept busy with a full course load of study. I had seven courses to keep up with that year: Religion, Latin, English, Algebra, American History, Speech and Music. I earned respectable grades in all these subjects, mostly Bs, with a couple Cs and As thrown in.

English was, of course, still my favorite subject, since the good School Sisters of Notre Dame had taught me well and given me a firm foundation in that subject. It was taught by Father Leo Rosloniac, who also taught Speech, and was the dreaded Dean of Discipline too. Father Leo was pretty demanding and maintained high standards in his classes, but also had a sly sense of humor and made it a point to get to know all his students. He was generally liked and respected by all the boys and young men at St. Joe's.

A couple of authentic report cards from St. Joseph's 1958 -1959 semesters.

Algebra was probably always the hardest subject for me, since my introduction to Algebra by Sister Mildred in eighth grade was less than helpful. Sister Mildred didn't understand algebra herself and merely gave it a dithering, cursory lip service, telling us we'd learn more about it in ninth grade. But my algebra teacher at St. Joe's, Father Joseph McKinney, was a patient, competent teacher, and I finally managed to get a basic grasp of the concepts under his tutelage and earned Bs and Cs in the class. (Father McKinney later went on to become an Auxiliary Bishop of the Grand Rapids Diocese.)

Father Robert Rose (who later became the Bishop of Grand Rapids) was my music teacher, and introduced us to the mysteries of Gregorian Chant, and also identified possible candidates for the choir. I never became very adept at reading music, but I had a passable singing voice and could usually quickly memorize necessary melody lines, so I quite enjoyed music class. And, having attended Mass all my life on practically a daily basis, Gregorian Chant and the Latin lyrics of the Mass were almost second nature to me. Before my voice changed, I had been a boy soprano in St. Philip's children's choir. But I was a bit too shy then to solo, so my brother Bob would sing with me on hymns like "Oh Lord I Am Not Worthy," or "Jesus in the Little Host." I loved singing in the seminary chapel along with the whole student body, and especially enjoyed hearing the choir when they performed the more complex pieces of Church music.

It is disappointing and even frustrating to me now, some forty-five years later, that I cannot remember many specific incidents, or any real defining moments from my one year at the seminary, except perhaps one. That moment came after I had been at St. Joe's only about a month. It was the first family visiting day, probably sometime in October. My mom and dad and Mary and Chris, my younger sister and brother, all came to visit, and brought a delicious picnic lunch that had no doubt been lovingly prepared. However, I was unable to really enjoy it. I've already mentioned how homesick I was during my early weeks at St. Joe's. By the time family day came around, I had decided I would go back home with my family that day. I simply missed my own home too much to stay any longer, so I was really looking forward to this day and to returning home. But I hadn't mentioned this plan in my letters home, so when I told my folks I wanted to come home with them, Mom and Dad were both taken by surprise. After a few uncomfortable moments of considering this (and consulting privately with Mom), Dad explained to me, as kindly as he possibly could, that coming to the seminary had been my decision and had required a lot of planning, expense and sacrifice, and he and Mom thought that I needed to abide by this earlier decision now and finish out the school year at St. Joe's.

Now, in retrospect, I know that Mom and Dad's rejection of my plan to quit the seminary was a wise one. It taught me a valuable life lesson about finishing what you begin – indeed, a concept they had always preached to all of their children. I know they didn't want to hurt me; that was the last thing they wanted to do. But at that moment, on that day, I was simply devastated. It was all I could do to hold back the tears, as I managed to choke down a token helping of of Mom's picnic lunch and sleepwalked through the motions of showing my family around the campus. I remember waving good-bye as they drove away, and then walking as fast as I could without running to the chapel, which was, blessedly, quite empty. Then all the pent-up tears and disappointment came rushing out and I cried and cried until I was all cried out. Then I prayed. I prayed for the strength to persevere. I prayed that I would do well and make my folks proud of me. But mostly I just prayed for God to help me just get through the rest of the year so I could get back home again for good. And then, miraculously, I felt much better. My homesickness was never a major problem after that day. I settled in and did my work and enjoyed my free time with my new friends, and made the most of every day at St. Joe's, because I knew that this year, my first year there, would also be my last. So, ironically, but perhaps prophetically, this was probably my defining moment at St. Joseph's, the moment I decided I just wasn't cut out to be a priest, but also the moment when I recognized that God would get me through whatever I had to do. I recognized, perhaps for the first time, the real power of prayer, something I still very much believe in.

Even though I only lasted a year at the seminary, it made a lasting impression on me, and not just in a religious sense or in matters of faith. The study habits inculcated at St. Joe's were to serve me in good stead throughout the rest of my high school years, as well as later on in college. We learned how to budget our time for all our subjects and also – further reinforcement of my father's credo – to get our work done *first, before* play or rest.

A Kent Elevator Education

And I did work, once I got back home. I was fifteen years old that summer, and my dad put me to work, both at the elevator and around the house, not because I'd washed out as a seminarian, but simply because Dad felt I was old enough and big enough to do a day's work, and he didn't want any of his kids lazing around just because it was summer. I had worked for Dad at the elevator before, off and on since I was about eleven or twelve, mostly doing odd jobs and sweeping up. One of my main responsibilities had been working at the seed counter where I would measure out, weigh and bag various garden seeds in quarter-pound, half-pound or pound-size paper sacks. Sweet corn was always a popular commodity for local gardeners. Over the years I probably weighed up and bagged hundreds, if not thousands of pounds of Alphagold, Golden Bantam, and other hybrid and popular varieties of the day, becoming very quick and adept at using the small, antiquated brass scale that sat on the counter in front of a bank of seed drawers that covered the wall behind.

I was also the PLO (permanent latrine orderly – remember *No Time for Sergeants*?) at the elevator in those early years, i.e. I cleaned the toilet, a job my mother had prepared me for at home – to a degree. I qualify that, because cleaning our bathroom at home was light duty compared to swamping out the elevator john, where the farmers would track mud and manure in and out, and often hawked tobacco juice, phlegm, or green gobs of viscous snot onto the floor or in and around the sink and toilet. In other words, it was a nasty job that no one else wanted, so I was usually elected, and eventually became inured to the filth. I went in, swabbed, mopped and brushed as quickly as possible, and got out.

Even Dad would occasionally be grossed out by these bachelor farmers' field-born habits of hygiene (or lack thereof). I remember him ducking his head and grimacing when one of these characters would lay a thumb against one nostril and hawk a hocker noisily out the other onto a freshly mopped floor right in front of the sales counter. Sometimes he would even say something, like, "Gee Christmas, John! Couldn't you do that outside?" Often as not though, the culprit would just peer quizically at him and wonder what all the fuss was about.

Often these rustic customers provided an unexpected source of mirth. One older fellow often complained of "prostrate" problems, which made it difficult for him to empty his bladder. He would remember nostalgically how, as a young man, his stream was strong and full and he could "piss higher than my head." Now he could only manage an intermittent dribble. "But it seems to be gettin' better," he'd say. "I can piss a little higher this year. Last year I used to dribble on my feet. This year I'm dribblin' on my knee."

Working at the Kent Elevator was often grueling and dirty work, but it was an education of sorts too. When I came back to work there the summer after my year at St. Joe's, I was "promoted" to helping out in the mill and warehouse. There, under the tutelage of the other men, I learned how to buck hundred pound bags of feed and grain, using my back and legs. I learned to run the mixer, where salt and molasses were added to the corn and oats the farmers brought in to be ground for cattle feed. I learned to tie a quick and efficient miller's knot on the burlap bags that held this mixture and other feeds. I learned to stack five or six hundred-pound bags of feed onto an iron handcart and muscle it up and down ramps and then load the bags into trucks or car trunks, or else re-stack the bags in the warehouse for storage and re-sale. I helped unload boxcars full of incredibly heavy small bags of Portland cement, or fifty-pound salt blocks. I unloaded flatcars of fragile red clay drainage tiles; hopper cars of coal; and boxcars filled with fertilizer.

In the process of doing all this often back-breaking and always exhausting work, I got to know the other workers better. Milt Steinhaus had been there the longest, and knew all the ins and outs of every job and tried to show me ny labor-saving (or back-saving) tricks he'd learned over the years. He had a sly, teasing sense of humor and wasn't above ragging or embarrassing any of the boss's sons. I remember one

Kent Elevator, early 50's, probably around Halloween. Note enormous pumpkin on steps.

particular occasion when we were all hanging around the penny peanut machine next to the loading dock door, and Milt wandered over to the sliding door that opened on the railroad siding, looked out, then ducked back and whispered over to me, "Tim, c'mere. Something you should see out here." Then he stepped back so I could peek out. Expecting to see a rabbit, or maybe a racoon, I peered around the doorframe and saw, not five feet away, the enormous bare bottom of a black woman, who was squatting up against the wall of the mill by the railroad tracks, taking a pee, dress hiked up around her waist and panties around her ankles. Embarrassed beyond words, I quickly yanked my head back inside, face beet red. Milt was bent over in near-silent laughter, hee-hee-ing to beat the band and slapping his knees, and all the other men were grinning widely at me. This became a story Milt loved to tell, always with a, "You shoulda seen Tim's face! He jumped back like he'd been burned! Hee-hee-hee!"

Don Churchill was one of the other men in the mill. His father, Mick Churchill, had been Dad's partner in the mill and seed business originally, but had sold his share to Dad after a few years. Don was an easy-going, seemingly happy-go-lucky sort of guy, always glad to pitch in on any job. He had an odd habit of smoking and chewing gum simultaneously. I asked him why he did both at once, and he told me, "The gum kills the taste of the tobacco." Hmm ... Okay, Don.

Another worker was Earl Walters, a short, graying, soft-spoken fellow already in his sixties. I used to get paired with Earl to deliver coal to homes in the surrounding area. Dad still had quite a flourishing coal business in the late fifties, as many of the older homes were still heated by coal furnaces. There was a sizeable coalyard out behind the mill and warehouse, close beside the tracks. Dad had an old Ford tractor with a front-end bucket we used to load the coal onto the dump truck. Once we arrived at the customer's house, it was my job to go position the portable chute from the truckbed into a basement window or the opening to the coal bin. Earl would then activate the dump mechanism of the truck, and I would climb up into the tilted bed and shovel the coal down into the chute, and scrape the coal out of the corners of the bed until all the coal was in the basement coal bin. It was a cold and very dirty job, but I kind of enjoyed riding in the truck to and from the jobs and feeling a bit self-important, knowing I was bringing warmth to these homes in the frigid months of winter. And Earl never failed to tell me what a good job I did, and how much he appreciated my help.

At the opposite end of the spectrum from deep winter and coal deliveries was high summer and wheat season. Wheat harvest was a labor intensive and very worrisome time for the farmers, and also for the wheat buyers at the grain elevators, businessmen like my dad. Prices were always in flux, so buyers and sellers alike tried their best to stay abreast of the rapidly changing prices to know when they could maximize their profits. Dampness and rot in wheat was a farmer's bugaboo. The higher the moisture content in the wheat, the less it was worth, so that factor was always measured and weighed in determining prices. There was a special mechanical device for checking moisture in a wheat sample, and Dad used this, but I also remember how he would often take a few grains from the sample and actually bite into the individual grains and *taste* the texture of the wheat. After years of experience, he had a pretty good sense of what was good product and what was bad. Farmers often argued and grumbled over wheat prices, but in the end, in general, they respected Dad's opinion and took what he could give them. After all, Dad was only a middleman; he had to make a profit too.

Once the wheat had been bought, cleaned and stored at the elevator, it would be shipped to other buyers – flour mills and food companies. That's where I came in. Once again, being essentially unskilled labor and junior man in the work force, I got the shittiest jobs that no one else wanted. In this case, it consisted of standing knee deep in wheat, amid swirling clouds of dust and chaff, in the middle of a boxcar. The dried wheat, which had been stored for a time in the upper reaches of the elevator storage bins, was then directed down a narrow chute into a boxcar for shipment to the final buyers. Situated in the center of the car was a mechanical auger to suck up the wheat and shoot it back into the far ends of the boxcar. However, the wheat poured into the car at such a rapid rate that the feed end of the auger would often plug up. My job was to stand at this initial juncture with a scoop shovel and try to regulate the intake feed and keep the augers working, so that the wheat would shoot smoothly back into both ends of the car.

Wheat in such volume is heavy, so it was hard work. It was also extremely dusty. I wore a kerchief tied over my nose and mouth, but I was a hay fever sufferer, so that didn't help much. After a half hour or so, my eyes and nose would be streaming tears and snot, and I would be wracked with sneezing. Periodically, I could close the chute and climb out and take a break, but not for long – time is money, especially during wheat harvest. I would trudge miserably up to the office where the bathroom was. Dad would look at my flushed face, snotty nose and streaming eyes, and shake his head, then tell me, "Go wash your face and blow your nose and get back out there. We have to get that car loaded and on its way."

This was essentially the usual treatment for my allergies – wash my face and blow my nose (and blow and blow and blow). In retrospect, observing all the children and adults who pay regular visits today to their doctors and specialists for allergy shots, it seems almost comical now, but it wasn't very funny at the time. I still suffer from seasonal allergies. But, from years of habit I suppose, my treatment is still the same – wash and blow. Oh, and by the way, if you ever thought your cream of wheat tasted just faintly of snot, now you know why.

RCHS: Geeks, Girls and Basketball

In the fall of 1959 I was back in school again – Reed City High School. It was a heady experience. For the first time since I was five years old and a beginner at Holdenville School, I was not starting my schoolday with morning Mass. What's more, I wasn't attending chapel four times a day anymore either. The strict regimentation that was St. Joseph's was over.

And there were girls. And you didn't have to peek through a line of trees or a chain link fence at these girls. They were all around you in the school hallways and in classes, and bumping up against you going up and down the stairs. You could smell their perfume and hairspray and soap and shampoo, and hear their laughter and their voices, with a softer timbre than boys' harsher voices and raucous laughter. It was glorious, and more than a little unnerving at first. It was new and largely uncharted territory to me.

I have to say, right up front, that I was never much of a ladies' man in high school. I would have liked to have been one, but I was just too darn shy. I was also too tall and skinny and wore thick glasses and had a face full of zits. You get the picture, I'm sure. All I needed was a plastic pocket protector full of ballpoint pens and pencils and I'd have been the classic geek. Hell, I *was* a geek, there's no escaping the fact. (Actually I'm not sure the word "geek" was around then. I think the correct term at that time was "dork.") I was six foot three, but only weighed about 160 pounds. I was still growing, so I was clumsy and uncoordinated. I was a mess.

But I really wanted to date. I think my last previous "date" (maybe my only one) had been in the seventh or eighth grade, when I took Maureen Milligan to see Elvis Presley in his first feature film, *Love Me Tender*. And I think Dickie Martz may have tagged along on that one. He was a year older than us, but an extremely pretty and effeminate boy. Anyway, it wasn't much of a date.

Reed Theater on East Upton, 1960.

I can vaguely remember my first official date, shortly after I started high school in Reed City. Her name was Donna Filley, and she was indeed a pretty little filly. She was a freshman in my biology class. Biology is usually a freshman class at RCHS, but, since I didn't take biology at St. Joe's, I was one of only a couple sophomores in the class, which may have given me a certain cachet, in spite of my geekiness – I was an "older man." And I was a new kid in school too, perhaps lending me a further air of mystery. An any rate, suffice it to say I got lucky. I really did, because Donna was much too pretty for a geek like me, with deep brown eyes and a cute figure. I asked her out to a Friday night movie at the Reed Theater, and she said yes. I was so happy and excited (but stayed outwardly cool, of course).

The Filleys lived in an upstairs apartment downtown, right next to the theater, so we didn't have far to walk. Walking was, after all, my only mode of transportation at the time.

If you're hoping for a heavy-breathing love scene here, don't hold your breath. Here's what I remember. I *don't* remember what the movie was. My big concerns were how to get my arm around the girl in the dark theater without being too obvious, and whether it would be too forward to hold hands on a first date. (Remember, I was a good Catholic boy.) I think I ended up managing both maneuvers, but what I remember most about that date was that the theater was pretty crowded, and just when I was starting to plan my next move, *some*body farted. No, it wasn't me. I appreciate a well-placed fart as much as the next guy, but this was *not* the place. And I don't really think it was Donna either. I'm not pointing any fingers, but *some*body must have had cabbage or beans for supper. At any rate, it sure spoiled any romantic mood we might have been working towards. There was no noise. It was one of those SBDs ("silent but deadly") that (as George Carlin once said) "coulda knocked a buzzard off a shitwagon."

We might have gone out for a coke at the drugstore or the Nestle Inn after the movie, but I don't think there was any kiss good-night. That fart had been the kiss of death for our date.

So that was my first date in high school. I didn't have a lot of dates, but they did get a *little* better. I know I developed a lot of crushes and spent a lot of time mooning over various girls, but never really did much about any of them. The weird thing about me and girls at that time was the way I idealized all of them. They weren't sex objects to me. I had not yet reached that predatory stage of the courting ritual. Girls were these soft, helpless things that were to be protected and held carefully and looked after. And also, just incidentally, they were very exciting to touch and just be close to. Maybe that's why girls weren't much attracted to me (in addition to my geekiness or dorkiness) – I just wasn't *dangerous* enough. Because let's face it, girls do seem to gravitate towards the dangerous sort of guys, who seem to exude an aura of sexuality. I didn't have "a aura," as Horshack would opine years later on *Welcome Back, Kotter*.

But I *was* tall. I stood out in the crowd between classes, when everyone was milling about in the halls. And on my very first day of school at RCHS I was approached by a short gentleman with a crewcut, obviously a faculty member. He was Dick Severance, the varsity basketball coach. He came right up to me and introduced himself and first asked my name, which I told him. Then he asked me, "Do you play basketball?" I said no, and he immediately said, "I'll teach you."

Thus began a three-year alliance, very rewarding for me, but probably mostly frustrating for poor Coach Severance. Because again, I'll admit from the start, I was never a great basketball player. But his singling me out, and his enthusiasm in teaching me was an enormous ego booster for a gangly geek fresh out of the seminary, and I have always been extremely grateful to him for all the time and attention he lavished on me.

RCHS Varsity Basketball Team, 1961. L to R: Coach Severance, J. Montague, F. DeVoe, R. Dolly, T. Bazzett, L. Ponce, S. Schmidt, G. Morningstar, Mgr. R. Hinkley. Bottom Row: P. Peffer, J. Whitman, G. Bluhm, G. Perdew, M. Scharlow, D. McKay, J. Stieg

I was a real beginner at basketball. As a kid, I'd shot baskets at a homemade backboard and hoop in our yard with my brothers, and had played a few pick-up games in the seminary gym, but my grasp of the game was pretty rudimentary, and my shooting and dribbling skills were abysmal. Coach Severance checked my class schedule and signed me out of my study hall period, took me to the unoccupied gym, and worked painstakingly with me individually, teaching me to shoot simple lay-up and jump shots, doing the rebounding for me himself and continually making suggestions on how to capitalize on my one court advantage, my height. His criticism was always constructive and his patience seemed limitless. He made me feel special and I would have done anything for him.

Unfortunately, I wasn't a natural. I was just as clumsy and uncoordinated on the court as I was in everything else. At around six foot three, I had gone through a huge growth spurt already in the past couple of years, and I wasn't done growing. I continued a slower growth until I was nineteen or twenty, finally stopping at six foot five and about 180 pounds.

I recognize that my height and weight back then are negligible, if not outright laughable, by today's basketball standards, but at that particular time I guess I represented Coach Severance's "great white hope," because, for the three years I played at Reed City, I was the tallest kid on the team.

I played center, but I was hardly the "center" of the team. I was always surrounded by much more talented athletes, some of whom had been playing ball together for several years by this time, both in sanctioned public school leagues and in summertime pick-up games. Since I had attended St. Philip's and then St. Joe's for the past nine years, I was an outsider, the "new kid on the block," and as such I was never quite accepted by the inner circle of local athletes who'd been playing together in the public schools all their lives. What happens to the "outsider" in this situation is that the "insiders" manage to very subtly exclude him – translation: they don't pass him the ball, except as a last resort. So couple that treatment with my own athletic ineptness (translation: I fumbled and stumbled a lot), and it becomes easy to see why I never really excelled at basketball.

Probably the best player for the Reed City Coyotes during my three years on the squad was Duane McKay, a red-headed kid from Hersey, who, at barely five and a half feet tall, played an extremely aggressive and hard-driving point guard. Duane had an intense, almost angry, competitive spirit, and wanted to win more than anything, a desire that was usually frustrated, as we didn't win that many games. He was a shooter, and was consistently our team's

RCHS Varsity Basketball Team, 1962. L-R front row: Coach Richard Severance, Lynn Pontz, Rex Dolley, Gary Steig. Back Row: Tim Bazzett, Dwight Gingrich, Wes Benzing, Phil Peffer, Duane McKay.

high scorer, in the high teens or twenties, and once scored 32 points in a game against Montague our senior year. Other standout players of the time were Steve Schmidt, Lynn Pontz, and, later, Garry Steig and Dwight Gingrich.

Number 35 in action, December 11, 1961.
Final score: Cadillac 76, Reed City 54.
Bazzett scored 15 points that night.

Although I never cracked that inner circle of good players, I did make a few lasting friends – players who, like me, played hard and did the best they could. Together we had our moments of greatness and, most important of all, we had fun. Rex Dolley was one of my best friends, on and off the court. He was an easy-going guy, quick with a joke or a laugh, and made allowances for my clumsiness and blunders on the court because we were friends. He was undoubtedly a better player than I was, but my height gave me an advantage, so we were fairly equal in our court accomplishments. Rex's biggest asset, at least in my eyes, was he was always "up." He wasn't a brooder, like Duane and Lynn could often be, particularly after a loss (and there were plenty of those). Even after an embarrassingly one-sided beating, you couldn't squelch Rex's spirit; he'd still have a joke or a song, and I was usually not far behind him.

My playing was uneven at best. I had my moments of glory though. My highest point output came my first year, while still a sophomore on the junior varsity, when I once scored 22 points. As a senior varsity player, I scored 15 in a loss to Cadillac, then 17 in a win over Shelby, but then my output dwindled and fluctuated anywhere between nothing and 12 points. My defensive play often redeemed me. In a close loss to Scottville, I scored a respectable 12 points, but also managed to almost shut down the normally high-scoring Scottville center, Ron Hansen, who managed only two points that night. And in a win over Evart that year I scored only two points, but ruled the boards with 17 rebounds. So, as I said, I did have my moments, and overall my high school basketball years left me with good memories, in spite of all the losses. I am most grateful to Coach Severance for teaching me the game and then letting me play and have fun.

Of course there was another benefit to being on the varsity. It was status. On game days the players had to dress up and could wear their letter sweaters or jackets. (Back then players always wore a dress shirt and tie with a blazer or sweater to games. It was de rigeur in those more civilized times.) The cheerleaders wore their uniforms to class on game days too. This custom created a sense of school pride and got the kids pumped up (at least theoretically). Often there would be pep rallies, where the players would all be introduced, and the coach would say a few words to the student body. (Pep rallies were often an occasion for pranks by school "bad boys" too. Probably everyone remembers the time some inflated prophylactics were hung in the doorways to the gym, bobbing gaily to greet the students as they assembled.)

The status or cachet afforded me as a varsity letterman (I also lettered in cross-country for two years) was only marginally helpful to me socially. After all, I was still a geek, and the minimal basketball shorts and jersey only served to emphasize my long skinny physique.

But I did have a few dates, most notably with Norian Layton, a new girl in school who was very cute, and also, incidentally, very well-endowed, as we used to say. Nori wasn't accepted by the circle of in-crowd girls, who treated her quite poorly, probably because she was new, and too attractive to boot. And she had all the boys interested, including some of the boyfriends of that in-crowd. Maybe I was a pity date from Nori's point of view, but if I was, I didn't mind. She was gorgeous and she was kind to me, and I enjoyed every minute of her company and basked in her reflected aura. (Yes, she *did* have "a aura.")

It was a short-lived relationship anyway, as Nori soon moved on to dating upperclassmen and "older men." (Did you ever notice that, how all the really hot girls your own age gravitated to older guys?

Didn't you just *hate* that?) One of these was, briefly, Doug Call, who lived with my family for a short time when his own people moved away during his senior year. (He was a classmate and friend of my brother Bob.) I liked and admired Doug, so it was a dilemma. Well, not really. It was Nori's choice, after all, not mine, and she was way out of my league to begin with. Later, she also dated Tom Moffatt, who was three or four years older and something of a basketball legend in Reed City, a natural athlete who exuded grace on the court, and who had a distinctive pigeon-toed shamble that I (and numerous other Moffatt wannabees) tried to emulate.

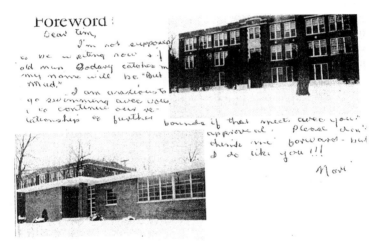

Maybe I shouldn't be too hard on myself regarding my short "relationship" with Nori. And no, it wasn't me who called it that. I probably couldn't have even defined "relationship" at the time. We were only sophomores, for cripe sake. But I recently found this lovely note in my 1960 *Coyote* yearbook and present it here for the record:

> *Dear Tim,*
> *I'm not supposed to be writing now, and if old man Bodary catches me my name will be "But Mud." I am anxious to go swimming avec vous & to continue our relationship to further bounds if that meets avec your approval. Please don't think me forward – but I do like you!!!*
> *Nori*

Nori, not only do I pardon your French, I do not think you were being forward either. Thank you for being my girl, if only for a very short time. It did wonders for this dork's adolescent ego. Alas, Nori and I never did go swimming together, and our "relationship" had run its course.

But I had other crushes too those last couple years of high school. I had some bad ones for a couple of cheerleaders, Sue Andresen and Marilyn Ochs, but they had boyfriends already, both football players. And there was Frances Perdew, who was Jerry Whitman's girl, and Jerry, although a year older than me, had been one of my closer friends ever since we played junior varsity basketball together. Fran was blonde and cute and full of fun. She and Jerry double-dated with Nori and me a couple times and we had a lot of fun.

There were also a few unspoken and unacted upon crushes on a few much younger girls, ones which made me feel vaguely guilty for even thinking about them. They were only a few years younger than me, but high school years can be like dog years. They yawn like wide chasms of time, absolutely uncrossable. There were a couple of JV cheerleaders, Connie Sadler and Patty Scharlow, whom I privately pined for. And even a bit younger, Karen Sahlin.

Karen's dad was an attorney in town and her family had a cottage on Indian Lake too, just around the bend from ours. You couldn't help noticing Karen those summers we spent at the lake. She was something of a tomboy, very athletic and competitive, and possessor of a firm, lithe little body that was a dark, honey-toned brown from hours spent in the sun and on the water, swimming, diving and water-skiing. By the time she was twelve, Karen was probably hands down one of the best water skiers on the lake, even better than the boys and young men in their teens and twenties who congregated around Ciermans' and Kings' docks on summer weekends to ski and race their souped-up speedboats up and down the lake. Karen had sun-blonde hair that I would describe as "sleek," as it was usually wet and pulled straight back in a pony-tail. She was the elusive, unattainable water nymph I could only watch from afar, always feeling slightly guilty for even being interested in such a "child." I suspect now that there were a lot of boys – and men – who also had their eyes on her, with the same mixed feelings of guilt and shame. Although she was probably completely unaware of it, Karen was the *Lolita* of Indian Lake for a few golden summers.

Were there any "fast" girls at RCHS? Well, probably, but none that *I* was personally acquainted with. I was still pretty much the good Catholic boy I'd been brought up to be, the ex-seminarian who put all girls and women on a pedestal. But there was, in my own class, Patty Brinker. I first noticed Patty at my Monday night CCD class during tenth grade. These Confraternity of Christian Doctrine courses were designed by the diocese to supplement or continue the religious education of kids who were attending public schools. Since St. Philip's only went to eighth grade, this meant all the Catholic high school students in Reed City. Patty Brinker didn't attend St. Philip's. She had always been a public school student, so I hadn't known her before. But while I was still a St. Philip's student I did notice the Brinkers, a large family from Hersey, who always attended Sunday Mass. Two of the older Brinker kids, Ronnie and Ruth, were twins, and were strikingly beautiful people; there's no other way to describe them. To my young eyes, Ruth looked like a movie star; she was that head-turningly beautiful. Patty was just a little sister, so I guess I had never really noticed her. But sometime when I wasn't looking, maybe that year I was away at the seminary, she blossomed, or budded, or *something*. By the time she turned fifteen, she was a real dish, with dark wavy hair, flashing mischievious eyes, and a dimpled smile that could reduce me to a puddle of nervous sweat.

With all these assets – and a few others too – Patty was something of a tease and a flirt. I mostly only witnessed her rather shameless maneuvering, as she lavished her wiles and considerable charms on the "cooler" boys in our classes, like Mike Scharlow or Ron Pegg, both football players. In an era of buttoned up Peter Pan collars, Patty was one of the few girls who might wear something scoop-necked, or would perhaps leave one more button undone at the top of her blouse, and might even lean in close near the boys, sometimes affording a glimpse of delicious decolettage. Maybe the more sophisticated, experienced guys could handle this kind of not-so-subtle teasing, but me? Instant embarrassment, blushing, incoherent stammers – puddle of sweat. Patty was Reed City High's answer to Gina Lollobrigida or Sophia Loren. She seemed that exotic and unattainable to me. Unattainable, but not unapproachable, for she was always unfailingly sweet and friendly to just about everyone, which only increased her charm. Truthfully, I don't think Patty was "fast." She was just gorgeous – the material that daydreams are made of. (Heavy sigh here.)

License to Drive,
or "Goober on Wheels"

Of course, one of the prime requirements for successful dating, then as now, was access to wheels. My sophomore year I turned sixteen, and also successfully completed the required Driver's Education course, and was ready to get my license. Two years earlier I hadn't been so sure though. That summer my brother Bob had just gotten his learner's permit, and was driving back to Indian Lake with Mom and a load of groceries in the car. While making the turn onto the Lake road from the Cedar Road, Bob suddenly, for no apparent reason, froze at the wheel, and failed to straighten out the wheels and continue up the hill. Instead he drove directly down into a five-foot deep drainage ditch, coming to an abrupt and jarring stop in the bottom of this ditch. The car did not turn over, and neither Bob nor Mom were injured, just very surprised to have ended up there.

Luckily, or un-luckily, depending on your point of view, I suppose, a Michigan state trooper was coming down the road right behind them. (Hey, maybe *that's* why Bob froze. He saw that police car in his rearview mirror!) The policeman stopped, helped them out of the car and took them to call a wrecker to pull the car out of the ditch. Amazingly, the car had sustained no major damage.

Nevertheless, my dad, being a reactionary excitable kind of guy in regard to major investments like automobiles, really went

Our 1958 Chevy parked next to the Elevator, circa 1960.

off at Bob that night when he got home for supper. Bob just hung his head and looked appropriately shamefaced and miserable. As a witness to this uproar and family drama, I listened fearfully to all of Dad's dire pronouncements about what *could* have happened due to Bob's inattention and carelessness, and silently vowed *never* to get a driver's license myself.

Thankfully, by the time I turned driving age, I'd forgotten this vow and was raring to go. I wanted the freedom of wheels. Unfortunately, Dad was not so anxious to add still another youthful driver to his insurance policy. Rich, Bill and Bob were already on it and had significantly increased his premiums. So he put me off and made excuses.

In the meantime, I had my learner's permit to practice, and I really needed practice, because our Driver's Ed car had been one with an automatic transmission. Our car, a 1958 Chevrolet Biscayne (in addition to being considered one of that year's ugliest models), was a manual transmission. Dad certainly wasn't going to take me practice driving, so Mom prevailed on my brothers, already licensed drivers, to teach me the mysteries of the clutch pedal and the "three on the tree" stick shift. I think Rich, Bill and Bob all had turns at taking me on practice runs. Rich even made the supreme sacrifice of letting me practice on his own car (but only once). Rich's car was the epitome of style and cool in 1960 (and still would be today). It was *the* car to have. It was a 1957 red and white Chevrolet Bel Air hardtop convertible with whitewalls,

128

Rich's '57 Chevy at Indian Lake, circa 1959.

mudflaps, a Continental kit spare, and twin glass-pack mufflers. Even kids today would call it *way* cool. Like I said, we only used his car as a learning vehicle once.

This was not surprising, since I was no cleverer than anyone else just learning to drive a stick shift. It takes some practice to find that exact pressure point required in the clutch mechanism, and to coordinate this with steering wheel, brake pedal and accelerator, all of which eventually comes together in a symphony of smooth shifting, turning, braking, passing, etc. Before you get it all right though, there is often much jerking, stalling, roaring engine, whiplash, and screeching of tires. Not to mention the screaming, cursing or condescending snide laughter of some sibling instructors.

Bill was probably the most patient of my teachers. He didn't yell at me much, and wasn't too upset by my initial ineptitude with the clutch. He used to take me over to Woodland Cemetery, at the top of Church Avenue, to crawl slowly about on the gravel trails there. I guess he figured I couldn't kill anyone where everybody was already dead. Smart thinking, Bill.

However, I do remember one particular incident there when he was teaching me how to back up, and I accidentally popped the clutch and lurched backward with considerable force into a tall old tombstone, then stalled, leaving the stone tilted precariously at about a sixty-degree angle. Afraid someone might have seen us, we got out of the car and looked guiltily around, but no one was in

Front and rear views of Mom and Dad's dream house at 355 West Church Avenue, custom built by Matt Mattzella and Sons, 1960.

sight, so we both put our shoulders to the stone and attempted to right it, but it was too heavy to budge, so Bill tactfully suggested we get the hell out of there pronto, and we did.

At any rate, after a few weeks of practice, I became adequately proficient at driving a stick shift, and felt ready to take my driving test and get my *real* license. Dad still wasn't ready though, and continued to put me off, until well into the summer when, unfortunately for Dad, he sustained a painful and disabling hernia. He was finally forced to enter the hospital to have the hernia surgically repaired. While he was still recuperating in the hospital, Mom took me over to the Sherriff's office, where I successfully passed my driving test and got my license. Dad learned of this only after the deed was done. Thanks, Mom.

So I was finally mobile. I had wheels, sort of. I didn't *own* a car, and wouldn't for quite a few years. I could borrow the family car only for special occasions or legitimate reasons, which was probably just as well, since I wasn't really a very good driver yet.

Case in point: later that summer I had another "secret" accident with Dad's car. But unlike the gravestone incident with Bill, I couldn't just flee the scene of this accident. I was working part-time at the mill that summer, and sometimes when business was slow, Dad would send me home to mow the lawn or wash the car. This particular time it was the latter job I was sent to do. We always washed the car by pulling it up onto a patch of lawn in front of our dining room window, between the open breezeway to the garage and our side-door porch. Dad didn't like to muddy up the driveway, and figured the runoff from washing the car could do double duty and water the grass there too. So, feeling quite

Dad in our 1960 Oldsmobile, circa 1962.

important about having the car all on my own, I dutifully nosed it up onto this patch of grass and got out to get the hose. But then I noticed that the rear end of the car was still hanging out in the drive, so I got back in and started the car to move it up a bit further onto the lawn, but I forgot to depress the clutch, causing the car to leap forward into the breezeway before stalling. It hit one of the support posts with a sickening crack, pushing the 4X4 post inward at an unnatural angle. I quickly restarted the car and backed it out of the breezeway, but the post remained bent in at the level of the car bumper, and was definitely cracked through. Horrified, I assessed the damage, trying to think – *How can I hide this*?

Practically running in circles, and with one eye on the time, I found a hammer and a piece of 2X4 lumber in the garage. Holding this board up against the inward bulge of the breezeway post, I carefully hammered it straight again, but the crack was still clearly visible. Flinging the board and hammer back onto the workbench, I quickly discovered a half-used gallon of matching white paint, found a paint brush, and thickly slathered the paint over the crack, covering it up. But then the rest of the post appeared dingy next to the new paint, so I quickly re-painted the whole post from roof to floor. Standing back to survey my work, it was quickly apparent that this post was much whiter than the other three supporting posts, so I hastily painted those posts too. Then I had to get a rag and some gasoline to clean up my paint spatters on the concrete floor of the breezeway. And there were quite a few. You have to picture all this frenzied activity taking place in a herky-jerky

Keystone Cops kind of fast-motion, because I was so terrified that Dad or someone else might show up at any moment and see what I had done, and I'd never be allowed to drive the car again. It was my own special version of Bob's driving into the ditch, my worst nightmare come to pass.

Finally, after also removing a smear of white paint from the car's bumper, I administered one of the world's fastest car washes, and got my sorry ass back to the elevator to work.

No one ever noticed our slightly whiter breezeway posts or the small dent in the car bumper, and I was very relieved when, not too long after that, Dad traded the car in on a new 1960 Oldsmobile, and later that fall we moved into our new house that had been built in the field between our old house and Grandpa and Grandma Bazzett's farm. As far as I was concerned, the timing of these events couldn't have been better.

That 1960 Olds was a vast improvement over the '58 Chevy, which was, incidentally, the last stick shift car Dad ever owned. The Olds was an automatic, and a sleek machine. Since I didn't have that many dates, I actually looked forward to Monday night CCD classes, which Dad let me have the car for. I developed a sudden concern for being not only punctual for class, but early. I would leave home fifteen or twenty minutes early for what was a five-minute drive. I would use this time to cruise the mean streets of downtown Reed City, often speeding up Lincoln Street in front of the high school, imagining how impressed my classmates (read: *girls*) would be if I had this car to drive to school every day. It was a short block past the school, so I would have to really stand on the brakes to make the stop at the end of the street. Dad never could figure out why that Olds needed a brake job after less than a year of driving it.

Sex Education
at the Ionia Free Fair

Although my social life still sucked, I did see my first real live (nearly) naked woman that summer I was sixteen. She was a burlesque dancer at the Ionia Free Fair. My brother Bob and his pal, Jim Mumy, were going to the fair, and somehow I got to tag along too. Bob and Jim had just graduated from high school, so I suppose neither really wanted me along, but maybe Mom sent me with Bob, hoping it would keep him out of any mischief. (Sorry, Mom. No such luck.) Jim was a really nice guy (a good Baptist boy), and probably didn't mind my tagging along, but I doubt that Bob felt the same. At any rate, we roamed around the fair, enjoying a few rides and scoping out girls, but once we saw that burlesque tent, I don't think there was ever any question in our dirty little minds that *that* was what we wanted to see. We circled back past the tent a few times, checking it out, and noticed that there was a sign posted at the door that stated that only patrons "18 and over" would be admitted, so Bob and Jim took me aside and cautioned me to "act older." They were both already eighteen, but chances were good that this was to be a first for them too.

Predictably, the barker selling the tickets couldn't have cared less how old we were, and took our money and waved us into the dark, smoky tent, which was filled with several rows of folding wooden chairs, with a small stage at the front. There were perhaps a dozen other patrons in the tent when the stage lights came up and some corny comedian came on to warm up the crowd. I can't remember whether he was funny or anything he might have said. I was too excited about seeing an actual stripper and things I'd only heard whispered about in the locker room.

The dancer's "name" was Desert Storm. She was a redhead, and to my young and lascivious eyes, quite a babe. A seedy-looking four-piece combo, heavy on bass and drums, started their schtick, and out she came, dressed in a filmy chiffon evening gown, spike heels and long, dressy gloves. Always the gloves, of course. They provide a tantalizing preview, the first things to come off – slow-ly peeled down the arm to the wrist, then, after delicately loosening one finger at a time, they are finally plucked daintily off and tossed aside where they float dreamily down to settle in a lacy heap on the floor, or perhaps slide lazily off the polished bald head of one of the musicians. All the time the bass and drums kept up a sinuous, booming rhythm. The three Reed City boys were mesmerized, hardly breathing. There was no question of acting cool anymore. I'm sure that to a man our eyes were wide, sweat was popping out on our foreheads, and our mouths hung slightly open with perhaps just a bit of saliva running down our chins.

Next came the gown, one shoulder strap pushed off, then the other, a slow graceful turnabout, then a shameless shimmy. Then, as if by magic, with the flick of an arm, the gown was gone, tossed aside, and here was this *woman*, swaying sinuously in just her *underwear*! Adam's apples bobbing, the Reed City boys gaped and drooled until, finally recovering a small shred of adolescent dignity, we joined the other anonymous patrons in that classic, timeless chant of the burlesque: "Take it off, Baby! Take it *awwll* off!" We were suddenly men among men. This was the real thing.

This Desert Storm knew her stuff. She didn't hurry. She knew the value of an-ti-ci-pa-tion, and, ever so slowly, and perfectly in time with the grinding, primitive beat, she peeled down her stockings and flicked away the filmy garter belt. Then, with that marvelous, wing-like motion that all women unconsciously know, she reached behind her back with both hands and unhooked her brassiere, that holy grail for teenage boys that we had all so irreverently referred to at times as "tit-slingers," "flopper-stoppers," or "over the shoulder boulder holders." Gracefully, shrugging her shoulders, the bra came away, and there "they" were, in *almost* all their glory. For the tittilation continued. Her nipples remained covered by gold lame stick-on pasties – pasties with a long "a," not to be confused with pasties with a short "a," a small meat and potatoes pie popular in Michigan's upper peninsula. Given the opportunity, however, at that moment probably any man in that tent would have eaten *those* pasties, short or long "a" be damned.

The last thing to come off were the gold lame panties, which had breakaway snaps and were flung aside with a flourish, revealing a tiny g-string. Following a few artful shimmies, bumps and grinds affording us breath-stopping, all-too-brief glimpses of her perfect white breasts and bottom, Ms. Desert Storm promenaded off the stage out of our lives (but into our hearts and memories) forever.

Afterward, emerging blinking into the bright Ionia afternoon sunlight with dry mouths and half-mast hard-ons, we were all too embarrassed to even meet each other's eyes. We didn't talk about the performance beyond a few wondering softly-voiced *Wow*s. It was simply too special, and I think we all felt a kind of unspoken reverence. Seedy though it all might seem in retrospect, we were changed "men." But perhaps the experience was best summed up for us by Bob, when he turned to me and said, "Don't tell Mom, OK?"

More High School Daze,
Smart & Stupid

Much of high school remains hazy in my memory. I suppose it's probably because my body was so ruled by raging hormones, fantasies and daydreams. Reality was often less interesting than my inner life. I remember identifying rather closely with the protagonist of Thurber's story, "The Secret Life of Walter Mitty," when we read it in Mrs. Croft's English class. I was a hopeless romantic and a dreamer. I didn't dream of deeds of derring-do though. I just gazed furtively at all the cute girls who swirled around the fringes of my everyday life at school, and imagined what it would be like to hold them close and feel their softness, to kiss them, to always say the right thing, to be pimple-less and handsome – to be *cool*. Because no matter how hard I tried, I know that I never quite achieved coolness. My clothes were never quite right. I had bad skin and crooked crowded teeth. I was practically tongue-tied in the presence of attractive girls. I wished to be like Steve Schmidt, with a gleaming perfect smile and blonde Nordic good looks, who had actually perfected that Tom Moffatt shamble, and exemplified grace on and off the basketball court. Or like Boyd Buerge, with his perfect upswept and sculpted DA, square masculine jaw, sharply creased chinos (with that little ivy-league buckle on the back) and mohair sweaters, and with Joyce McChesney (one of the most perfectly beautiful girls in school) on his arm.

But I was never to break into that charmed circle. Instead I was part of a second-level fringe group of kids, more like myself. I ran with Rex Dolley and Art Gerhardt, with Chuck George, Don Truax, Chris Tiel, and Jim Baar. Some of these guys (Don, Chris and Jim) were real scholastic whiz-kids and classic overachievers, and were into school clubs and student government. But the rest of us – Rex, Art, Chuck and I – were more into goofing off and having fun.

More than a few times this got me into trouble, especially in the math and science classes which I still detested, but were part of the pre-packaged college prep cululululum. In Algebra II, Rex and Art and I would sometimes sing snatches of currently popular songs or harmonize softly (or at least hum annoyingly) when we were supposed to be working on problems. This didn't sit well with our teacher, Mrs. Toman, who finally sent us to the office, where we were sentenced to a few hours of detention. I don't know if detention is still a discipline tool in public schools, but it never seemed particularly effective to me. That extra hour or two after school spent in the company of other "bad boys" (there were rarely any girls in the detention room) just afforded me time to finish my homework (a truly nerdy thing to do, in the opinion of any *real* delinquents doing time there). My biggest worry was keeping my criminal behavior from my mom, but I usually managed to come up with a plausible excuse for my late arrival home.

Another time, Mr. Kilmer threw me out of Physics class for sleeping. The thing was, I *wasn't* sleeping. It's true I was sitting with my head down and eyes closed, but I was not asleep. So I was promptly filled that righteous indignation that only an unjustly accused adolescent can muster. I made the mistake of arguing with the teacher, telling him I *was not sleeping*. He threw me

Loren Kilmer

Mr. Kilmer - chemistry and physics teacher.

137

out anyway, and I went blustering angrily over to the office to complain bitterly to our principal, Mr. Messner, telling him I was quitting Physics. I hated it anyway. Sensing the delicacy of the situation, Mr. Messner managed to calm me down, diplomatically pointing out that I needed that class to complete my curriculum and to graduate. Then he sent me to study hall to cool my heels. The next day, somewhat chastened, I went back to Physics class and nothing more was said of the incident. For the rest of the year there was an uneasy truce between Mr. Kilmer and me. But for a short time I enjoyed a minor and fleeting celebrity among my goof-off friends for having faced down Mr. Kilmer in class and then complaining about him to the principal. (What an insufferable jerk I was.)

I was also involved in another shenanigan which to this day leaves me feeling vaguely ashamed. We had a young student teacher in Math class, a Mr. Bryce. He was, I'm sure, doing the best he could to teach us seniors the mysteries of Calculus and Trigonometry, but I still hated and dreaded math in any form. Mr. Bryce, a small man, had a habit of hoisting himself up to sit on the windowsill, facing into our third floor classroom, and swinging his feet while we were working on problems. One particularly fine spring day, Keith Eichenberg and I spontaneously decided to have a little fun with Mr. Bryce, so we casually sidled up to him, one on each side, firmly grasped his arms and slowly pushed him out the open window and held him there, as he gripped the sill with his knees, eyes wide with alarm, stuttering in protest. Grinning good-naturedly, we asked him if we were going to have any homework for the weekend. When he managed to stutter out that, no, we wouldn't have any homework, we eased him back into the room, and he managed to regain his composure. The whole class had seen what happened. Poor Mr. Bryce was embarrassed beyond words. He must have been, because he didn't send us to the office, and he didn't report the incident, as far as I know. Maybe that's why I still feel guilty. It was a moment of pure thuggery, and we got away with it. What in the hell were we *thinking*? We could have been *expelled*! And what if we'd *dropped* him? *Geez*, we were stupid! Anyway, Mr. Bryce, wherever you are, I apologize profoundly, and sincerely hope you went on to an illustrious career in teaching and the shaping of young minds. It wasn't you, really. It was just hormones out of control again.

Fortunately, there were a couple subjects I did enjoy in high school. I liked Latin, a subject I'd begun to study at St. Joe's, and did well in, so I took a second year of it at RCHS. Latin was the first foreign language I ever studied, and it was an ideal basis for the study of other languages (and I did study a few other languages later in my life). My Latin teacher at Reed City High was Mrs. Beth Fischer, a very elegant, coiffed and proper lady, who insisted on good behavior and

ELIZABETH FISCHER

Mrs. Fischer - French and Latin teacher.

proper pronunciation in her class. I can't say I remember much Latin, other than the standard "amo, amas, amat" (I love, you love, he-she-it loves), and something about "All Gaul is divided into three parts." But I seemed to have a natural curiosity and a talent for things linguistic, and enjoyed the challenge of translating. I probably had a decided edge over many of the students due to my seminary background, where Latin was especially emphasized, since it was the official language of the Church. At any rate, it was a course that came easy and I enjoyed it.

The subject I enjoyed most was English, because you got to read new things, and, in spite of my raging hormones and sometime bad behavior, I remained a voracious reader. In addition to this, the good School Sisters of Notre Dame had given me a firm foundation in grammar and the mechanics of our native tongue. (Thank you, Sister Justin, for all those hours of diagramming sentences.)

DOROTHY WOLFINGER

Mrs. Wolfinger - English teacher.

Probably my two favorite teachers during my years at Reed City High were Mrs. Dorothy Wolfinger and Mrs. Margaret Croft, both English teachers. My first exposure to Mrs. Wolfinger, a very short (under five feet), round, effervescent woman who loved teaching and loved "all her kids" (perhaps because she had no children of her own), came in the tenth grade. She taught composition and grammar, and took an immediate liking to me and my writing. It probably helped that I already understood most of the concepts she was tasked with teaching. She was often apalled (as was I) at the linguistic ignorance of many of the ninth and tenth graders who passed through her classroom. This is not to say she didn't treat all her students kindly and fairly. She did. She simply appreciated the occasional student (usually St. Philip products) who actually understood what constituted a complete sentence and the difference, say, between and adjective and an adverb.

Mrs. Wolfinger also encouraged me in my writing, although my "style" at that time was highly derivative, depending on what I was reading (or watching) at the time. One of my compositions that first year was a slight essay on Lower Slobbovia and its strange residents. I was a fan of Al Capp's *Li'l Abner* comic strip in the Sunday funnies at the time. Another piece I submitted was a stylistic takeoff on the clipped, curt voice-over narrative of Jack Webb's Detective Sergeant Joe Friday character, from the popular TV series, *Dragnet*. Not very original, I know, but apparently more imaginative and a cut above what Mrs. Wolfinger was used to in student essays. She would also often read my compositions aloud to the class. This, however, could be a double-edged sword. While it did afford me a certain celebrity as a budding "writer" (and did impress some of the girls), it also marked me as a kind of nerd and suckup to the less desirable hoodlum elements in the class, those guys who never did any homework, and skulked about the school entries or near the dumpsters with lit cigarettes concealed in their cupped hands. True, I probably shouldn't have been concerned with what these types thought, but I was. These guys did have a certain glamour of their own kind, and I wanted their approval too. So if something I wrote could make them laugh, all the better.

For whatever reasons, Mrs. Wolfinger liked me, and, since she and Margaret Croft were close friends, when I entered Mrs. Croft's classes my junior and senior years, she was already predisposed to like me too. And I immediately liked Mrs. Croft. She was very different from Mrs. Wolfinger, both in appearance and in her teaching style. She was tall and angular, and had children already grown. She was from Nebraska, and spoke with a unique midwestern twang that was easy for her students to imitate and make fun of. I even succumbed to that temptation myself on occasion, even though I loved Mrs. Croft and her class. She had a very dry wit and highly developed sense of humor, and wasn't above using a bit of barbed sarcasm to keep her rowdier students in line. I was something of a cutup myself, and she cut me down a few times too, so I quickly learned to respect her and wisely cleaned up my act.

Margaret Croft

Mrs. Croft - English teacher.

Our anthology and reading lists were pretty typical of high school English classes anywhere, but I actually enjoyed most of the things we read. The authors included Jack London, F. Scott Fitzgerald, Hemingway, Thurber, George Eliot, Robert Frost, Emily Dickinson, Vachel Lindsay, Shakespeare and Faulkner. Many of the selections we read by these and other authors were just excerpts from longer works or short stories. I was probably the rare exception in students exposed to a smattering of classic world literature in that I would follow up. After reading "To Build a Fire," I went to the library and sampled other London books. I'd already read *Call of the Wild* and *White Fang*, so I read *Sea Wolf*, something quite different. I struggled through Faulkner's short novel, *The Bear*, then devoured Hemingway's *A Farewell to Arms* and a whole collection of his northern Michigan Nick Adams stories.

I began sampling other current adult literature, and discovered *The Catcher in the Rye* (my brother Bill had a copy). I read James Michener's *Hawaii* and Hilton's *Good-bye, Mr. Chips.* My mother subscribed to *Reader's Digest* , and we also received the *Reader's Digest Condensed Books*, which I read or sampled regularly. In short, I was discovering a whole world of literature, and reveling in it, and Mrs. Croft played a large part in this discovery.

My English classes were welcome, healing oases in the last year or two of high school, parched with the dry formulas, tables and rote memorizations of chemistry, physics, higher mathematics, history and government. In spite of my aversion for all subjects mathematical or scientific, I managed to get through all of them, and even maintained a B average throughout my years at RCHS. For this I should probably thank my dad and all the priests who taught me good study habits at St. Joseph's Seminary. The credo was constant: work first, *then* play. My study habits saved me. I graduated with honors (just barely), fourteenth in a class of eighty-four.

The Crystal Ball and the Senior Prom, or "Twisting the Night Away"

But it wasn't all just classroom drudgery or shenanigans that last year of school. I also managed to attend a couple premiere social events.

One of these was the Crystal Ball. This was not a school dance, but a much-touted and exclusive community-sponsored event. It was a semi-formal coat and tie dinner-dance held at Miller Auditorium at the airport just north of town. It featured a sit-down dinner catered by the Osceola Hotel, and music was provided by the Les Elgart Orchestra. In anticipation of this fete, I had even purchased Elgart's latest album, which was a collection of big band arrangements of the Twist.

Ah, "the Twist." I just have to digress here, so hang in there, I'll get back to my story. The Twist was a unique dance craze of the early sixties that was simply unparalleled. It began as a lowly, none-too-successful rhythm and blues number penned and recorded by Hank Ballard and his band, The Midniters. Never heard of them? Well, then how about Ernest Evans, aka Chubby Checker, who covered the tune in 1960 and leapt to the top of the charts and stayed there for an incredibly long time, and spawned a host of imitators and carbon copy songs, like Joey Dee's "Peppermint Twist," or Gary U.S. Bonds' "Dear Lady Twist."

The unusual thing about "The Twist" and its equally popular followup, "Let's Twist Again," is that in 1962, two years after their initial successes, they ruled the top forty charts once again, throughout the spring and summer of my senior year.

The Twist wasn't just a record or a dance, it was a whole culture. Kids today would say it was "way cool." It *ruled.* It was such a simple dance that virtually anyone could do it, but you could also add an infinite number of stylistic and specialized variations of your own. If you could dry your ass with two hands and a towel, you could Twist. If you could walk and chew gum, you could Twist.

Of course I bought Chubby Checker's album and played it to death practicing my moves, often twisting non-stop through the entire side of the album, six songs. (But six songs then rarely would exceed fifteen minutes in an era when a pop song's optimum duration was two to two and a half minutes.) I remember one spring night when several of us gathered at Ruth Dykema's house on East Todd and literally twisted the night away. It was such a fun-filled, sweaty evening. Thank you, Ruthie, for providing the venue. I didn't get to that many parties in high school, and yours was really a blast.

But where was I? Oh yes, the Crystal Ball, with Les Elgart and his Orchestra. Elgart was a society band at the time, and was on the road with about fifteen musicians, so having a band like this providing the music was a really big deal in Reed City. I bought Elgart's then-current album, *The Twist Goes to College,* and used it to practice my dancing with for a month or two before the big night.

Who did I take? I hope she still remembers it as fondly as I do. I was "between" girl friends at the time. Shit, who am I kidding? I never had any steady girl friends in high school. I was the perennial geek, remember? I asked Jan Layton, Nori's younger sister. She was a sophomore my senior year, and I'd had my eye on her for some time. (Don't you just *hate* it when the *older* guys hit on the cute young girls?) She was petite and cute, a type I'd always been a sucker for. I sweated for a while about asking her, not certain whether she'd go with me, since for a guy like me there was no such thing as a "sure thing." But she accepted and seemed pretty excited. Well, she probably *was* excited. After all, this was an adult function, not just a school dance. There really weren't that many high school kids going. I know *I* sure was excited.

Since I still didn't own a car, we double dated with my brother Bob (by then a student in the pharmacy program at Ferris State) and Maureen, who were a pretty steady item by that time. Bob had bought Grandpa Whalen's last car, after Grandpa died in 1960. It was a fairly pristine 1956 Chevy, and we washed and waxed it to a high gloss for the big night so we could arrive in gleaming splendor.

Miller Auditorium was a town treasure back in the sixties, still fairly new. Jim Miller was the founder and owner of Miller Industries, probably one of the town's biggest employers. Miller's manufactured various glass and aluminum products and had made Jim Miller a millionaire. The airport and auditorium, with an adjoining park and pond (complete with a small island and a resident pair of swans) and dam, were just a couple of Miller's philanthropic contributions back to his community. One of his hobbies was collecting player pianos and other mechanical music-making devices and oddities, which were on display throughout the auditorium. The hall itself boasted a stage and a high vaulted ceiling. It also had its own well-equipped kitchen, restrooms, and an enormous gleaming terazzo floor that could be used for audience seating, dining or dancing.

The night of the ball this space was utilized about equally for dining and dancing. The event took its name from a large lighted "crystal" globe that hung suspended over the dance floor and revolved slowly, giving off multi-colored, prismatic lights with an intoxicating, strobe-like effect. It was magical. Under its glamorous glow even the most awkward dancer appeared graceful. A good thing – some of us needed all the help we could get.

The cooks and catering staff from the hotel provided a sumptuous and delectable dinner for the evening. Then Mr. Elgart struck up the band, and the dancing began. That night this Reed City boy rubbed shoulders with the cream of local society, as we all "twisted the night away." We dined, we danced, and had a wonderful, magical evening, and I think I may have even gotten to kiss the girl good-night that time.

Like her sister, Jan Layton also left me a note about that night in the 1962 *Coyote,* so I'm giving her equal time.

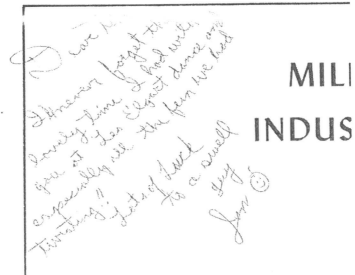

MIL

INDUS

Miller Industries, sponsor of the Crystal Ball, and Jan's yearbook note, 1962.

Dear Tim,
I'll never forget the lovely time I had with you at
[the] Les Elgart dance and especially all the fun
we had twisting!!
                    Lots of luck to a swell guy,
                                          Jan

I also attended the Senior Prom that last year of high school. I mention the Crystal Ball first, because I think it was more fun for me. There were fewer expectations and I had a pretty little girl on my arm, who probably had as much fun as I did. It was a civic function, and didn't carry all the baggage of tradition that comes with a prom. I didn't have any real girl friend my senior year, so I kind of dreaded the approach of the prom. I wanted to go, since, as everyone kept badgering me (especially the girls): "You'll only ever have one senior prom, and if you don't go, you'll always regret it." Well, I kind of doubt that that's really true, especially where guys are concerned, but it had the desired effect at the time. There were a number of girls in my circle of friends who made me their "good will project" in regard to the prom. Or perhaps I should say they used me to effect their real aim: to find a prom date for Susan Martz.

I had known Susan Martz since grade school days at St. Philip's. She and her older brother Richard (or "Dickie") were a little different, but everyone was used to them, and didn't really give a lot of thought to their "different-ness." Richard was a very "pretty" boy. There's just no other way to put it. He had striking dark brown eyes, delicate features, thick dark hair, and a creamily perfect skin and complexion. I think he may have even had a beauty mark or two. He had a way of walking up on his toes that also set him apart. I think his physical beauty and unmistakably effeminate mannerisms isolated him from the rest of the herd, and I'm sure life was not easy for Richard, growing up in Reed City. I never really knew him very well; I'm not sure anyone did. At any rate, he left town soon after he graduated from high school, and I don't know if he ever came back.

OSCEOLA HOTEL

AND COFFEE SHOP
"EAT WELL AND
SLEEP WELL"

Reed City, Michigan

Susan was the other side of the coin. She wasn't homely. She wasn't ugly. She was, well, "handsome," I guess you could say. Her eyes were a bright blue and she had a small dark mole on one cheek that would have been a beauty mark on a prettier, more feminine girl (or on her brother), but on Susan it was just a mole. She was more solidly built than her brother, and perhaps even was a bit broader in the shoulders, but with slim, boyish hips.

It's difficult for me to remember Susan and describe her with any real accuracy, because she was always just "there," part of a crowd of girls that I grew up with, and, although she was a nice-enough girl, I never took much notice of her. She wasn't the kind of girl you'd get a crush on. She was tomboy-ish, but not flamboyantly. She had an unobtrusively masculine kind of walk. She didn't sway or float or sashay the way a lot of girls did. She planted her feet firmly and squarely and got where she was going. She was athletic in a time when girls didn't really have a forum for athleticism, at least not in high school. There was no real organized sports program for girls in the early sixties. They had gym classes, of course, in which they played some games. And they had GAA, the Girls Athletic Association, an extra-curricular organization, but I'm not sure what that accomplished, or what it was for. Susan was a jock when there just weren't many acceptable outlets for girl jocks in high school. But she was always part of a circle of girls throughout elementary and high school, and seemed to have plenty of girl friends. To me she always seemed very quiet and non-assertive. Other girls liked her, and boys didn't dislike her. No, Susan was always just "there."

Anyway, a bunch of her friends – Maureen, Liz Erbes, Ruth Dykema, Diane Fatum, Fran Perdew and others (she *did* have a lot of friends) – decided early on to find Susan a date for the prom, because no one, particularly a girl, should miss out on the senior prom. Since I was part of the group, and had no steady girl friend, and cleaned up reasonably well, I became the logical candidate, and became the focus of much overt and covert campaigning. I was mooning a bit at the time over Sue Andresen, a cheerleader, but she still had an older, steady beau, Jerry McGinnis, so that was pretty much hopeless.

To make a long story short, I buckled under the pressure, and asked Susan Martz to the prom. I'm not sure she really wanted to go to the prom, with me or anyone else, but she too knuckled under to overwhelming peer pressure, and accepted my offer. So neither of us missed the hallowed senior prom.

We doubled with Bob and Maureen. (I *know.* I know I said we never really got along, but Bob had the *car.*) Susan was all decked out in up-do, make-up, and an off-the-shoulder gown of frilly organdy, or some such kind of layered material, and looked distinctly uncomfortable most of the evening. But we smiled, we danced, we went through all the appropriate motions. We went to Bauer's in Big Rapids to eat afterward (or was it before?). We even went out to Indian Lake after the dance was over for a little parking. Boy was *that* awkward! (Geez, Bob, what were you *thinking?*) We got through the night though. Having said all this, I also have to say that I'm grateful to Susan for going with me to the prom. It may not have been truly memorable, but at least we could both tell people, years later, "Yeah, of course I went to my prom."

The prom, by the way, was held in our high school gymnasium, and I think Susan and I, and no doubt a few other shanghaied couples, had as much or more fun decorating the gym for the dance than we actually had at the dance itself. After all, how many teenagers actually enjoy getting all dressed up in coats and ties, or formals and stockings and long-line strapless bras, or any of that other special equipment required by such events? Most kids today go off to their proms in rented tuxes and stretch limos and spend hundreds of dollars on the night, dining and dancing at some impersonal venue miles from their school. For our prom, we wore our best Sunday clothes, polished up the family sedan or our own second-hand junker, and hung crepe paper streamers, aluminum foil stars and paper moons in the school gym or cafeteria, a homely venue that became just a little more special to us after prom night. Even today, I can walk through our old high school gym (now part of the upper elementary school, and targeted for demolition if some people have their way) and remember prom nights past, not to mention dozens of pep rallies, lunch time sock hops and basketball games. But I digress, I know.

The A&P, Trimming Trees,
and Naked Women

One other significant thing that occurred my senior year was that I quit working for my dad at the elevator and took a part-time job at the A&P grocery store at the northwest corner of Chestnut and Upton. (For those who don't remember the A&P, or the Great Atlantic and Pacific Tea Company grocery chain, it has since morphed into the Super Fresh chain of food stores.) I had helped out at the Kent Elevator after school and on Saturdays ever since I was eleven or twelve, and had always thought of this "job" as an extension of my home life. But for the last couple of years I had chafed a bit at working for Dad, who wasn't much for lavishing praise on his kids. I never seemed to be able to do things quite good enough to suit him, and I became increasingly sensitive to his jibes and criticism. (Anyone who has ever had to work for a parent will probably understand what I mean.) And I suppose I just wanted a bit more independence too. I was at that age. I don't know if Dad was hurt or disappointed when I took another job. I don't think so. I think he may even have been a bit pleased that I took the initiative and found a job on my own. He just wanted all his kids to know the value of working.

I think the real blow to Dad came a year or so later, when my oldest brother Rich enlisted in the Army when the draft was breathing down his neck. Dad had been grooming Rich for years to take over the business when he retired. He'd even sent Rich to Michigan State, where he'd gotten a degree in elevator management and agriculture. But apparently Rich had been looking, consciously or subconsciously, for a way out of Reed City, because he never really came back home again. The Army trained him to repair and install various types of high-tech electronics gear, and from that beginning he fashioned a whole career, which afforded him opportunities to travel all over the world. Come back to Reed City to work in the mill? Fat chance. "How you gonna keep 'em down on the farm," and all that.

My new job at A&P seemed like a step up to me. I wore a white shirt and a clip-on plaid bow-tie to work, where I stocked shelves, unloaded freight, and bagged and toted groceries. I also did the "cleanup in aisle five" kind of stuff whenever necessary. I started work there shortly after my pal Keith Eichenberg did, so we got to work together quite often, another plus. Our boss was a young fellow named Bernie. I mean *really young*, only in his early twenties. He'd started out as a stock boy like us, and worked his way up to store manager in very short order. He was already married with a couple of kids, but still looked very boyish. Bernie was a hustler, very organized and driven, but he was still enough of a kid that he could be prevailed upon, on a hot afternoon, to "accidentally" drop a watermelon from an incoming shipment, which we could enjoy eating, sitting in the walk-in cooler, once everything else was unloaded.

Tim and Bob and the "Blue Bomb," summer 1962. Wearing my A&P work clothes: white shirt with clip-on plaid bow-tie. Checking for stray boogers before work.

I worked hard at the A&P, but it was a congenial atmosphere and the other workers liked me. There was Bernie, of course, our young boss, with his floppy blonde surfer-boy hair. And Brandy Mellberg was our meat cutter, but could probably do any job in the store, since he'd been there so long. He was also chief of our local volunteer fire department, so whenever the siren sounded atop the firehouse a block over, on Higbee, Brandy would tear off his apron and rush off to other more important duties. And there was Floss Earnest, the head cashier and resident "mom," albeit a very attractive one. She kept Keith and me in line, and we loved it. Floss was very pretty, as was her younger sister, Pat Trombley, who, as Keith said, "had a pair of headlights that would stop a deer dead in its tracks." Yes, those Trombley girls were lovely to look at.

My job at the A&P wasn't my first job working for someone other than Dad. For parts of two summers I worked on tree farms, trimming Christmas trees. The first time I was sixteen, and joined a crew hired by young David Kilmer, the second son of Dr. Paul B. Kilmer. Each morning the crew of four or five kids gathered at Dr. Kilmer's house at the corner of Sears and Upton (conveniently located right next to the hospital), and young David ("young" to differentiate him from his uncle, Dr. David Kilmer, who had just begun practicing in Reed City) would load us all into a pickup and haul us north to a tree farm located somewhere near Cadillac. My first day I brought an old pair of shrubbery shears borrowed from my grandpa, but they quickly dulled, and weren't very efficient. It took too long to do all that two-handed clipping as you worked your way around each tree. Young Dave must have noticed this too, because the second day he issued each of us a razor-sharp Army surplus machete, and demonstrated to us the proper way to use it, making clean diagonal slashes from the top of the tree down, as he worked his way quickly around it. He also gave each of us a small mechanical counter to wear on our belts, to keep an accurate count of how many trees we trimmed each day.

I'm not sure the machetes were a good idea, considering we were all just teenagers, prone to goofing off. The machetes, as opposed to pruning shears, made us all feel a bit more manly and swashbuckling, prompting a few foolish mock sword-fights back in the concealment of the trees. Fortunately no one got hurt, and the machetes certainly did speed up the trimming process. But it was hot, boring work for the most part, and we tried to amuse ourselves however we could, once the initial novelty of the machetes wore off. We became quite expert at creating a shapely, conical tree, and took some pride in that, and competed to see who could trim the most trees in a day's time, something the boss encouraged, as long as we didn't mutilate ourselves or any trees in the process.

The following summer I trimmed trees again, this time on a smaller farm out west of town near Hawkins. It was owned by Bud Rosencrans, a fellow

RCHS Cross Country Team, 1961. L-R (top row): Rex Dolley, Tim Bazzett, Larry Williams. (bottom row) Phil Roggow, Coach Dale Clark, Glenn Bluhm.

from downstate somewhere, who only showed up occasionally after his initial walkthrough of the acreage with us, when he explained what he wanted done and showed us the boundaries of the farm. I worked that summer with a friend from school, Glenn Bluhm. We'd played basketball together on the junior varsity the previous winter and become pretty good friends. Glenn was probably one of the shortest kids on the team, but handled the ball well and was a scrapper on the court. We were also on the cross-country team for a couple years too. Glenn had his own car and he picked me up each morning that summer by around 5:30. We started so early because we quickly found out that it was no fun working in the extreme heat of the late afternoon, so we would usually knock off by three o'clock or so. Even then, those afternoon hours could be hellishly hot, as the sun beat down on us, and I have to admit that we did occasionally retreat to a shady spot and half-snooze or goof off, keeping one eye out for the boss, who would sometimes stop by unannounced, to check on our progress. On the whole, however, I'd say we worked pretty hard, and managed to work our way through all the trees in about a month's time, just the two of us, largely unsupervised. So we made a few bucks and still had some vacation time left.

One other highlight of that summer was a "nature" film that played at the Big Rapids Drive-In Theater. Actually, it was a seedy B-film about a couple of bank-robbers who take refuge from the law at a nudist camp. It was called *Hide-out in the Sun*. Somehow the word got out about this film, and I think every horny teenage boy (is that redundant?) in a thirty or forty mile radius was at the drive-in those couple of nights it was playing. *Nekkid women* – playing tennis and volleyball, for cripes sake! All that bouncing and bobbling and even full frontal nudity – something completely unheard of in the early sixties. After chafing under those Legion of Decency movie guidelines throughout my childhood, I could hardly pass up an opportunity like this, so Glen and I and a few other guys piled into his car one hot summer night, picked up a bag of fifteen cent hamburgers from the Satellite Drive-In restaurant for sustenance, and went to further our education. I will admit it wasn't as guiltily satisfying as the exotic dancer Desert Storm, but at that age we figured you could never know too much about the human body – and knowledge is a good thing, right?

Smoking, Drinking and Other Stupid Stunts

There were other ways those last couple years of high school that I attempted, mostly unsuccessfully, to accelerate this growing up thing. I took up smoking. I wasn't a regular or heavy smoker. Hell, I probably wasn't even very good at it. I was kind of like President Clinton – I didn't really inhale. Inhaling made me feel kind of sick or set me off in a coughing jag. I was more of a "social" smoker. I enjoyed that air of sophistication that smoking supposedly conferred on you. You have to understand that this was still the age of rampant and unscrupulous advertising by tobacco companies, and all those jingles we were bombarded with every day on radio and television had their desired effect. "Winston tastes good, like a cigarette should." "LSMFT – Lucky Strike means fine tobacco." Or "I'd walk a mile for a Camel." And that Marlboro Man was, after all, such a rugged, good-looking stud, wasn't he? Didn't you just wanna be like him, a chick magnet?

It wasn't the first time I'd tried cigarettes. When I was only twelve or thirteen, and those hormones were just starting to percolate, I knew there must be something better than those candy cigarettes (remember *those?* Madison Avenue was really on to something there, teaching *little* kids how cool it was to go around with a cigarette hanging out of their mouths) that would make me seem more "cool." So I started picking up the longer butts you could find anywhere along the streets or in the roads back then, filched a match book or a few kitchen matches, and would fire up these re-cycled butts out behind the garage or the barn. Anyone who does smoke knows how terrible a re-lit butt can smell, and taste. But it was what I had to work with at the time, and boy, did I feel cool. I took to carrying a matchbook in my pocket and would search the gutters and along the roadside for likely-looking butts on my way home from school in the afternoon, walking up Church Street. Finding one, I would light up and exhale a stream of rank-smelling but sophisticated smoke with a sigh of satisfaction. By the time I reached eighth grade, I'd become bold enough to occasionally buy a whole pack of smokes from a machine that stood outside the Gulf gas station (after first checking carefully to see that no one was watching). I came to prefer the newer, more obscure brands, like Hit Parade, Spud, or Newports. The menthol-flavored ones were best, I thought, because they tasted less like tobacco, and seemed easier on my youthful throat and tender lung tissue. Smoking was something to be indulged in rather furtively at that age, so I didn't do it often, only when I needed to feel a bit more adult. As a vice, in those times, it was perhaps a bit more socially acceptable than jerking off. In today's atmosphere of anti-smoking mania and sexual permissiveness, probably the reverse is true. One of my favorite anti-smoking anecdotes comes from an old Steve Martin bit. Someone supposedly once asked him, "Do you mind if I smoke?" To which Martin replied, "Why of course not. Do you mind if I *fart?*"

At any rate, I discontinued smoking altogether for a couple years, starting when I attended St. Joe's, although it certainly wasn't because of the good example of others there. All the upperclassmen, and most of the faculty too, smoked like chimneys. Then, when I was about seventeen, I took up the habit again, discovering the somewhat questionable pleasure of Wolf Bros. Rum-Soaked Crookettes, a rather foul-smelling twisted little cigar. I mean, how could we resist the appeal of something that combined two vices – tobacco and alcohol? A few of my friends and I would quite often buy a pack of these nasty little buggers and drive around smoking them and feeling adult.

About this same time, I also tried – just *once* – a long black evil-looking cigar, called, I think, a Wheeler Bros. My brother Bob and I were scrubbing and waxing the floor of Bonsall's Drugs one night after store hours. (Bob was a regular part-time employee at Bonsall's.) We decided to sample one of these black beauties out of the glass tobacco display case, so we lit one up to share. Boy, was that thing strong! After just a few puffs, I was sure I was going to throw up, although I managed not to. That single experiment cured me of any aspirations to real cee-gar smoking.

I also experimented a little with the teenager's drug of choice of that era – alcohol. Well, beer, anyway. And it really was only a little, too. I think it was the fall of my senior year when Jack Hurst and I boosted ourselves through an unlocked window in our cottage on Indian Lake and helped ourselves to a few of Dad's beers that had been left in the refrigerator. The brand was Pfeiffer's, a beer that is no longer made. In fact, when we drank it, it tasted so flat that I wonder if it may have already been an obsolete beer, even then. Dad wasn't much of a drinker, and sometimes beer would sit in the refrigerator for months (maybe even *years*). Anyway, it wasn't very good, and didn't even provide much of a buzz for us underage thrill-seekers. Yeah, I was a big time drinker all right – about like Dad was. But it seemed like a cool, "rebel" kind of thing to do at the time.

But James Dean I certainly was not. No, I was a small-town good Catholic boy through and through, as were many of my close friends. As teenagers, we entertained ourselves in simple ways.

As an example, there was a kind of outdoor parlour game we indulged in on lazy summer days. All you needed was a broom. Take a standard long-handled kitchen broom, then stand with your feet spread at about shoulder-width. Place the end of the broom-handle on your chin and look straight up the broomstick at the broomstraw end, up in the air over your head. You can hold onto the broom handle with both hands to support it, as you focus your gaze intently up the stick at the straws. Then, keeping your eyes on the straw-end, turn yourself completely in a circle approximately fifteen times. Once

Still another stupid broomstick trick. summer 1962.

you've completed these revolutions, quickly lay the broom down in front of you and jump over it. That's it. That's the whole game. Sound stupid? Sound easy? Well then, before you read any further, put the book down and go outside in the yard and try it ... No, that's okay. Go ahead. I'll wait ...

Okay, while a few of my idiot readers are outside in the yard hurting themselves, I'll explain why this can be a pretty challenging little game. Because after you've turned yourself around a dozen or more times while staring straight up into the sky, you're so damn dizzy you can barely stand upright, let alone lay something down and leap over it. Instead you end up lurching uncontrollably sideways and slamming yourself into the ground, or whatever else is there to stop you. I remember introducing this game at an adult party about ten years ago, when most of the party-goers were a little bit schnockered, and our host, Tom Hall, did a quick disdainful dozen or so turns, determined to show me what a *stupid* game this was, threw down the broom, then hurled himself full-force sideways into a rosebush. *Ouch!* Sorry, Tom. It's obviously a lot more fun watching someone else try to do this trick than to do it yourself. But, strangely enough, there are usually a few diehards in the crowd who think there must be some trick to doing this, and will try it over and over, smashing themselves repeatedly into the ground (or any nearby shrubbery). As kids, I think we probably got more of a buzz from spinning ourselves around and trying this trick than we could have gotten from drinking a whole case of Pfeiffer's.

In addition to "jump the broomstick," we would also play "kick the broomstick." Again, all you needed was a broom, a sense of fun, and an infinite supply of gullibility. Stand upright with your left leg crossed in front of your right, both feet on the ground. Hold the broom upright, business end down and resting on the toes of your right foot. Then, kicking with your right foot, try to kick the broom as far as you can. Whoever can kick it the farthest is the winner. (Okay, you same idiots can go outside and try this now.)

Of course, distance and winning are not really issues in this game either, since, if you really give it your all, and kick out with all your might and main (you *fool!*), you will also kick your crossed-over left leg out from under you and immediately fall flat on your ass. The real fun is in finding a fresh "pigeon" who's never seen or done this trick, carefully explaining the rules to him, and then watching him make a fool of himself. Actually that's the main point of both the broomstick games.

I know these games sound pretty juvenile, and they are. Younger kids, who don't bruise so easily, really have fun with these games. The truth is these are both really ancient games that my dad taught me, but not until I was already in high school, so that's when I introduced the games to my friends, and we made the rounds with them one summer, always looking for "fresh meat." I would still recommend these games anywhere you have a group of kids who need to burn off some energy. But do them outside on the lawn, where there's plenty of room to lurch around and fall down and make a really proper fool of yourself, not in the living room or family room – too many sharp-edged objects and furniture to fall into.

Ah, I know – the dumb things we did (and do) for a little fun. Dad used to say, "It doesn't take much to tickle a small mind." And there's a lot of truth to that, but you take your fun wherever you can find it.

One of the funnier things I remember happening one summer involved my brother Bob. It was that first summer he had his car, the '56 Chevy he bought from Grandma Whalen after Grandpa died. He was real proud of that car, which he christened "The Blue Bomb," and spent a lot of time washing and waxing and polishing it. I did the same thing when I got my own car a few years later. It's a guy thing. I once read a psychological explanation for this when I was in college. In layman's terms, it basically said that for a young man, a big long shiny car was like an extension of his dick, and the bigger, longer and shinier it was, the better. So does that mean that when you used to drive to the park on Sundays and park your car in the shade to polish it, along with a half a dozen or more other guys doing the same thing there, you were taking part in a kind of subliminal circle jerk?

I'm digressing, I know, but I just had to get that in there. Anyway, one fine summer Sunday afternoon, Bob had his Chevy all shined up and spiffy-looking and was cruising around town a little and looking for some action on the chick front. He took along his pal Jim Mumy, who was riding shotgun beside him up front, and Jerry Whitman and I were in the back seat. (I can't remember

Studly Ferris letterman Bob Bazzett with his prized "Blue Bomb" circa 1963.

how I got to go along, but I'm just glad that I did.) Bob was freshly showered and dressed in clean clothes and wearing his Ferris letter jacket and just generally looking and feeling very stud-muffinly. As we cruised east on Todd, we spied what can only be described as a "vision." Geri Schmidt was out in her driveway in a white two-piece bathing suit washing her car. How can I get across to you, gentle readers, what an absolutely stunning beauty Geri Schmidt was, back in that summer of '61? I can't. But take my word for it, she was a BABE in capital letters, with a drop-dead Coppertone tan, a perfect Pepsodent smile and Breck-beautiful hair. Bob crossed over to the curb by her driveway, and suavely hailed Geri, who came over to talk. Bob was cool, he was a master of chit-chat and small talk, but Geri kept her distance and somehow managed to resist his charm, a small fleeting smile on her lips. There was a reason for this, and the rest of us in the car, watching Bob put his moves on Geri, soon realized what it was. Bob had a small, flaky green booger fluttering just inside his right nostril, which appeared and disappeared as he breathed. Geri was trying her best not to watch this, but it was almost impossible, since, once you'd noticed it, you couldn't take your eyes off it. Jim, Jerry and I all started breaking up, snorting, laughing and guffawing. Bob, completely oblivious to his minute hygienic flaw, and trying not to show his irritation with our mysterious boorishness, continued to attempt to sweet-talk Geri, asking if she'd like to go for a ride. Smiling herself by now, she begged off, saying she had to finish washing the car and had some chores to do around the house. Face turning red, Bob accepted this as graciously as possible, then, driving off, exploded furiously at all of us, "What in the *HELL* are you assholes *laughing* about?!" Almost in unison, we all shouted back at him, laughing uproariously by this time, "You've got a BOOGER hangin' outa your nose!"

Hey, like I said, you take your fun wherever you find it. Sometimes it's the little things that make you laugh. And it was only a *little* booger, Bob.

While I'm on the subject, although Bob and I had our differences, we *weren't* sworn enemies, or anything so bad as all that. We were just different. And to give Bob credit, he was a very popular guy during his scant two years at RCHS. As a matter of fact, his senior classmates voted him most popular boy *and* the most likely to succeed – and he did. And I'm happy for him too. We've gotten along just fine for the past thirty years or so. (Of course it probably didn't hurt that we lived about a thousand miles apart for most of that time.)

ity High

This Certifies That

Timothy J. Bazzett

the requirements for graduation from the Reed City

Faculty and approved by the Board of Education

Diploma

Given at Reed City, in the State of Michigan

seventh day of June A.D. 1962

Graduation – and Gone

I was having fun and I wasn't really feeling very serious about my life that final year of high school, a time when many kids are carefully considering college and career paths. I had some college applications lying around the house from Ferris and Central, but I could never seem to make myself sit down and fill one out. I was even too lazy to send out any graduation announcements, until Mom got mad and made me do it. My list was pretty short, just my grandparents and my uncles and aunts, and then, just to kind of piss off my folks (and also perhaps a little curious as to whether I'd get a response), I also sent off an announcement to President Kennedy and his missus. I'll be damned if I didn't receive an engraved congratulatory message from Jack and Jackie a couple months later, something I've treasured and kept for my book of memories.

Nope, during my senior year at RCHS I was more interested in just enjoying myself, and this attitude was apparently all too obvious to my parents, who began gently pressuring me to think about what I would do with my life. Dad's constant refrain at this time was, "Well, if you're not going to college, then you'll have to get a job." Neither option sounded like much fun to me, so I began casting about for alternative choices, and I soon found a solution. I'd show Dad. I wouldn't go to college *or* get a job. I'd join the Army. And so I did.

It would be nice if I could say here that I enlisted because I was inspired by JFK's words, "Ask not what your country can do for you, but what you can do for your country." But I'd be fibbing. I joined the Army on an impulse.

One day after school I made a visit to the local Army recruiter in his cubby-hole office near the Mackinaw Trail restaurant and listened to his sales talk, learned of the delayed entry program, and signed my name. I was officially an Army recruit and would leave for active duty at the end of September. I hadn't consulted with anyone, and when I told my parents what I had done, they were horrified. They'd just lost Rich to the Army less than a year ago, and my impulsive enlistment hit them pretty hard, I guess. I didn't see what all the fuss was about. I just figured I'd solved the vexing problem of what I would do after high school. And, in a manner of speaking, I had. I was such an innocent, however, I had no idea what I was in for. Come September, I would learn for myself what a sheltered and idyllic life I had led in Reed City.

Following this decision, my final days in school and subsequent graduation seemed pretty anticlimactic. Graduation was held with all the usual pomp and ceremony at Miller Auditorium in early June, 1962. After shedding our caps and gowns, Keith Eichenberg and I put in a brief appearance at a graduation party at Chuck George's place, then went driving aimlessly around town and out through the surrounding countryside in his Ford, talking about nothing of consequence and smoking up a pack of Wolf Bros. Crookettes. Keith already had a job secured at the Reed City Tool and Die, and planned to marry the following year, when his girlfriend Dianne graduated from high school. His future seemed to be all mapped out and planned. Mine was kind of a question mark.

That summer following graduation I continued to work as many hours as I could get at the A&P, and spent part of my time in town and some time out at the lake too, but I was becoming increasingly restless and was anxious for the rest of my life to begin. Finally, on September 25, 1962, I boarded the North Star Line bus south for Detroit, where I would be sworn into the United States Army.

For this Reed City boy, the great adventure of life was about to begin. But that's another story – and I'm working on it.

Junior Rotarians

FIRST ROW, Left to Right: Earl Vincent, Chuck George, Tim Bazzett, Chris Tiel, Sponsor, Mr. Messner, and John Howe. STANDING: Glenn Bluhm, Craig Kilmer, Michael Keelean, Michael Teesdale, Lynn Pontz, Doug Johnson, Rex Dolley, Phil Peffer, Jerry Ruppert, Tom Andresen, Ron LeBaron, and Roland Lasch.

Two clubs I actually joined my senior year at RCHS.

Varsity Club

FIRST ROW, Left to Right: Wayne Hitzemann, Phil Peffer, James Baar, Glenn Bluhm, Chris Tiel, Rex Dolley, Advisors, Mr. Severance and Mr. Shook. SECOND ROW: Dan Stinger, Larry Sims, Craig Clark, Tim Bazzett, Doug Johnson, Tom Andresen, Jim Martz, and Lynn Pontz.

Congratulations on your graduation.
The President joins me in extending warm
good wishes to you always.

Jacqueline Kennedy

Acknowledgements

I would like to specially thank my son, Scott Bazzett, a tremendously gifted graphic artist and designer, who turned my scribblings and a box of old photos and papers into a strikingly attractive package. Without his considerable efforts, a labor of love, this book would probably not have happened.

Thank you also to my mother, Daisy Bazzett, and my brother, John Christopher Bazzett, for sharing their memories, for proof-reading and for their constant encouragement. And thanks too to my son, Jeffrey Bazzett, and my daughter, Susan Bazzett, for urging me to "just do it" – write!

Additional thanks go to Carol Yost Andres of Andres Computer Supplies for her assistance in duplicating certain materials; to Elizabeth Marek and Shelly Mix of St. Philip Neri Church for allowing me access to parish photo archives; and to the friendly and helpful staff of the Reed City Public Library.

Finally, I would like to thank all my friends and classmates from Holdenville and St. Philip Schools, St. Joseph Seminary, and especially RCHS. You were there. This book is for you too.

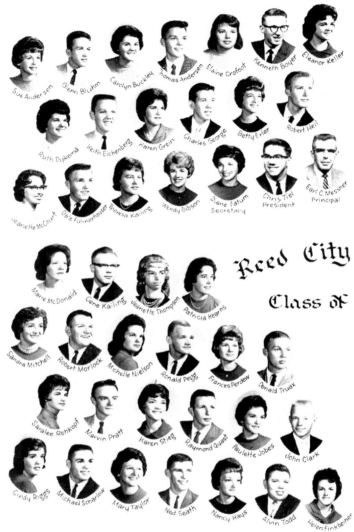

Sue Andersen
Glenn Bluhm
Carolyn Buckley
Thomas Andersen
Elaine Crofoot
Kenneth Boyer
Eleanor Keller

Ruth Dykema
Keith Eichenberg
Karen Grein
Charles George
Betty Erler
Robert Heil

Jeanette McCourt
Dale Fulmerhouser
Theresa Kailing
Wendy Gibson
Diane Fatum
Secretary
Chris Tiel
President
Earl C. Messner
Principal

Reed City

Class of

Marie McDonald
Gene Kailing
Jeanette Thompson
Patricia Kearns

Sandra Mitchell
Robert Morlock
Michelle Nielson
Ronald Pego
Frances Perdew
Donald Truax

Saralee Renkopf
Marvin Pratt
Karen Stieg
Raymond Quast
Paulette Jobes
John Clark

Cindy Riggs
Michael Scharlow
Mary Taylor
Ned Seath
Nancy Hays
Alvin Todd
Helen Finkbeiner

Patricia Porterfield

166

Marilyn Ochs
Jack Hurst
Karen Bitler
Lynn Ponitz
Patricia Brinker
Elmer Franklin
Fern Benzing

Arthur Gerhardt
Carolyn Crane
Wayne Hitzemann
Gloria Clementshaw
Jack Bates
Linda Fleischhauer

Godfrey T Norman
Superintendent
James Baar
Vice President
Elizabeth Erbes
Treasurer
Perry Allen
Cheryl Goodburn
Jeffrey Dibble
Josephine Kaminski

High School
1962

Darlene Pratt
Norian Layton
Rex Dolley
Judy Lehr

Daniel Stinger
Marlene Lobdell
Timothy Bazzett
Carolyn Holmquist
Douglas Johnson
Darlene Hinkley

Floyd DeVoe
Maureen Milligan
Earl Vincent
Susan Marth
Ronald Stieg
Vonne McDonald

Barbara Battle
Duane McKay
Sally Wetherell
Leon Saladin
Delores Stieg
Richard Sutherlund
Jane Seelhoff

H.A. Powell Studios
MICHIGAN · OHIO

167

Soldier Boy, Part 2 of *Reed City Boy*, is available now.

To order send check or money order for $16.00 made payable to TJ Bazzett to:

PO Box 282
Reed City, MI 49677-0282

(Michigan residents add 6% sales tax)

For more information, visit us online at:
www.rathole.com/SoldierBoy

ABOUT THE AUTHOR

Timothy James Bazzett was born in 1944. He holds degrees from
Ferris State, Central Michigan and Eastern Michigan Universities.
He taught English for five years at Monroe County Community
College and served eight years in the U.S. Army. He is retired from
the Department of Defense and lives with his wife and two dogs in
Michigan, where he continues to work on his memoirs.

PART 1

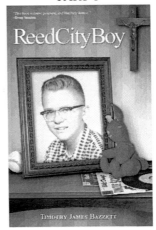

PART 2

Watch for PART 3 in 2006

Pinhead:
A LOVE STORY